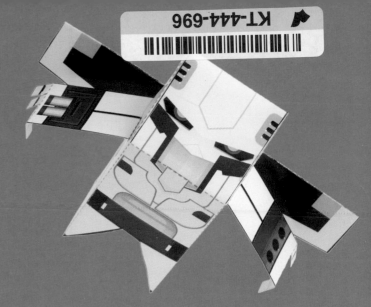

CONSTRUCT YOUR OWN

PaPeR ROBOTS

FOLd and GLue 35 amazing androids

JAMES RONALd LO

CICO BOOKS

LONDON NEW YORK

DEDICATION

To Diego, Storm, and Summer for the ideas.

To Mars for the unsolicited, yet necessary, mean comments.

To Lei for the inspiration.

Published in 2012 by CICO Books
An imprint of Ryland Peters & Small Ltd
20–21 Jockey's Fields
London WC1R 4BW

519 Broadway, 5th Floor
New York, NY 10012

www.cicobooks.com

10 9 8 7 6 5 4 3 2 1

Text © James Ronald Lo 2012
Design and photography © CICO Books 2012

A CIP catalog record for this book is available from the Library of Congress and the British Library.

ISBN: 978 1 908170 27 9

Printed in China

Design concept: Paul Tilby
Design: Jerry Goldie
Editor: Robin Gurdon
Photographer: Geoff Dann
Template illustrator: James Ronald Lo
Step illustrator: Stephen Dew

For digital editions, visit
www.cicobooks.com/apps.php

contents

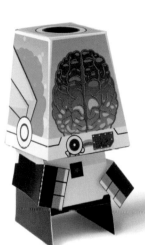

the templates 80

INTRODUCTION

paper toys, to me, are an art form with
no boundaries.

Any artist (as we all are in some form or another) with a computer
(sometimes even without one), a love for crafts, and some free time
can design a paper toy. All you need is an idea, some card stock,
glue, and a pair of scissors—and you're good to go.

Paper toys needn't just be appreciated from afar. They are three-
dimensional so you are encouraged to touch, customize, and build
them. The creator interacts with the "viewer" in so many levels. In fact,
the viewer is not just a viewer but also becomes closely involved in
the creation process as a paper toy must first be built
to be fully appreciated.

Paper toys are also very accessible; you can
upload a template online and
anyone in the world with an internet
connection can download your toy
and build it. You don't even have to
leave home to enjoy it!

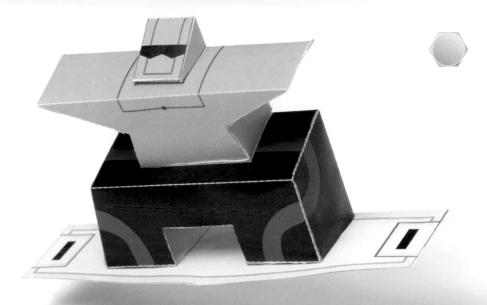

I came across the world of paper toys completely by accident. I was looking for a creative outlet, something that was different but crafts-related, so I went online to look for ideas and inspiration. I came across sites that featured origami, cartoons, as well as custom LEGO and vinyl toys and found them all to be absolutely fantastic, all very inspiring. Eventually, I stumbled upon a paper toy site and was amazed at what people did with paper. From there I got hooked and started designing my own toys, then even put up a blog (www.papertoyadventures.com) to share my "experiments" with the world. Through that blog I've interacted with so many great people who were kind enough to post a comment or two.

Now you have this book in your hands and you're reading it—yet another form of interaction!

I do hope you have fun assembling the toys in this book, perhaps even more than I had designing them!

James

TIPS 'N' TRICKS:
TOP PAPER TOY ASSEMBLY TOOLS AND HOW BEST TO USE THEM

i thought it would be a good idea to share the tools i use and some tips on how to make the most of them. hopefully you will find it useful.

Craft Knife/Cutter: When cutting ensure that the blade is very sharp. Using a fresh blade means your cuts are always "full and clean." If you use a dull edge, your cuts sometimes won't slice through the paper completely in a single stroke which means that whether you use a number of strokes or just tear it off you will destroy the neatness and edge quality of your paper toy.

Scissors: I wasn't a big fan of these until recently—I used to NOT use scissors at all. Normally, I'd cut up a paper toy using just a knife because scissors can be very inaccurate. I'd say it's nearly impossible to cut a 100% straight line with them as your hands tend to move around in different angles while you snip away. Needless to say, this is entirely my view so don't worry if you disagree! As mentioned, recently I've learned the benefits of using a nice pair of scissors—they are the easiest implement to use for non-linear cuts while knives are best for straight ones.

Adhesive: For best results use white PVA but do not apply it directly onto the toy from the bottle. Instead squeeze a small amount onto a piece of scrap paper and then use a second piece to apply the adhesive to the toy.

Tweezers: These are available in many different shapes and sizes. Use to hold together those hard to reach places.

Self-healing Cutting Mat: Use to protect your desk from your craft knife or cutter.

Steel Ruler: Sometimes referred to as a "steel edge," it is vital for cutting straight lines. Plastic or wooden rulers just won't do—you tend to make nicks in their edges and then end up cutting wobbly lines.

Old Credit Card/Protractor/Extra Ruler/Business Card/any flat, stiff board: Used in tandem with a ruler for folding straight edges.

Pencil/Pen: For applying quick and easy guidelines and especially useful when prototyping. Use a mechanical pencil if you want to be accurate and clean (you can erase the lead markings later) and use any other type of pencil or pen if accuracy isn't important. Ball point pens are messy, felt-tipped pens are better—but you'll have to wait for the ink to dry else you run the risk of having ink smudges all over the place.

HOW I CUT, FOLD, and GLUE

although the robots in this book come perforated and pre-creased. i want to explain how i do the three main activities of making paper toys: cutting, folding, and gluing. that way, once you've made all the ones in this book, you can move on and make some more!

HOW to CUT

This stage is pretty simple. You'll need a cutting mat, steel ruler and cutter or craft knife if the template requires. Place the cutting mat on a flat surface and place the steel ruler over the template to ensure you cut in a straight line, using it even when cutting very short lines. I hold the cutter like a pen, but this isn't for everyone, so just choose the way that feels most comfortable to you.

HOW to FOLD

Here, I use a ruler and a flat piece of sturdy card stock to create neat and exact folds.
Place the template on a flat surface and then the ruler on top, positioning it along the fold line (1). Push the card stock under the template from the outside until it slides up against the ruler (2) then lift the outer edge of the card stock to fold the template, using the ruler as a guide (3).

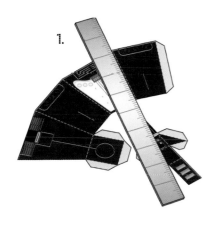

1.

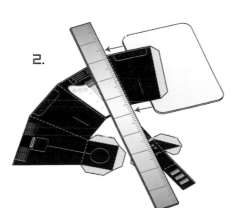

2.

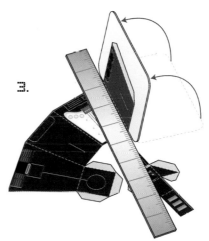

3.

HOW to GLUE

Squeeze a dab of glue onto a piece of scrap card stock (4) and then use a second piece as a "paintbrush" to apply the adhesive on the area to be glued (5). This allows the adhesive to dry faster, plus you avoid "squeezing out" any excess glue from the applied area. To finish, just hold the pieces together for a few seconds to dry. Sometimes, especially for tight spots, I use tweezers to clamp the two sides together.

4.

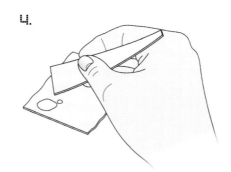

5.

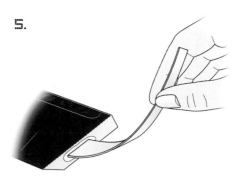

PROFESSOR NICOLO SPARK
the father

Prof. Spark is the leading inventor in Robot City. He specializes in robotics and artificial intelligence. The professor travels around the world giving talks about his many discoveries and inventions but whenever he gets the chance he works in his laboratory at the manor so he can spend as much time with his family as possible.

CONSTRUCTION INSTRUCTIONS

DIFFICULTY RATING

1. Detach all the templates from page 81.

2. Prefold all creases marked with a dotted white line to shape the model.

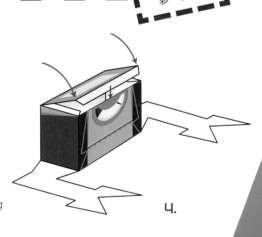

3. Start by assembling the head, gluing tabs 1a–7a underneath the corresponding edges.

4. Next assemble the body, sticking the tabs under the marked edges with glue.

5. Assemble the legs and both feet in the same way.

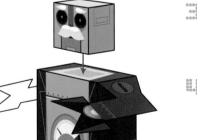

6. Attach the head to the body, gluing 29a to 29b, then glue 30a to 30b to join the legs to the body and finally add the feet, gluing 31a and 32a to 31b and 32b.

angelica spark

the mother

Necessity is the mother of invention, and Mrs Spark is the main source of Prof. Spark's inspirations. As she goes about managing Spark Manor, she comes up with new ideas to help her go about her chores. She tells the professor about all of them, and he turns the ideas into robots for her.

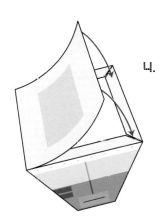

DIFFICULTY RATING

CONSTRUCTION INSTRUCTIONS

1. Detach the templates from page 83.

2. Prefold all creases and press out the slits on the side of the body where the arms will go.

3. Assemble the head, gluing tabs 1a–5a under their respective edges.

4. Make up the body, first gluing tab 6a behind 6b before folding down the top, 7a, and finishing with the bottom, 8a.

4.

5. Assemble the legs, folding down the front and back before gluing tabs 9a–12a against 9b–12b to hold them in place.

6. Attach the head to the body by gluing the sides 13a and 13b together then fix the legs to the body at point 14.

7. Finish by attaching the arms through the slits of the body.

6.

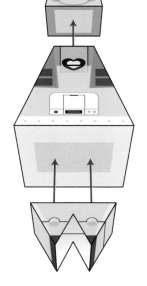

TEN
the surfer son

Anti-gravity surfing is the second most popular sport in Robot City after wrestling. Ten won the recent surfing championship. He is famous for creating the "Hang Ten" surfing move, where he hangs for 10 seconds in midair without an anti-gravity board.

CONSTRUCTION INSTRUCTIONS

DIFFICULTY RATING

1. Detach all four templates from page 85.

2. Prefold all creases, making the basic shapes of the different parts of the robot.

3. Assemble the legs, gluing tabs 1a–8a under their corresponding edges.

4. Assemble the body, gluing tabs 9a–13a under their corresponding edges before turning over the end flaps and gluing tabs 14a–17a in place behind edges 14b–17b.

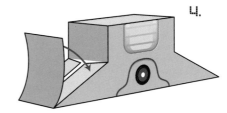
4.

5. Assemble the head, gluing all tabs under the relevant edges.

6. Create the hoverboard by folding it in half along the crease and sticking sides 23a and 23b together with glue.

7. Join the four parts together to make the surfer, sticking the head to the body at point 21, the body to the legs at point 22 and the body to the hoverboard at points 24 and 25.

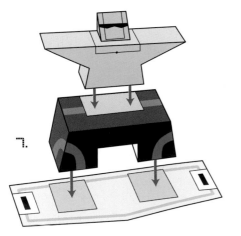
7.

ANNAMATRON
the Daughter

Annamatron was Professor Spark's very first creation. He developed this robot during his first year in the Robotics Academy. The golden heart on its chest shows that it was an experiment to prove that robots can have feelings.

CONSTRUCTION INSTRUCTIONS

DIFFICULTY RATING

3.

1. Detach the templates from page 87.

2. Prefold all the creases and press out the slits where the arms will go.

3. Assemble the head, gluing tabs 1a–7a under the corresponding edges.

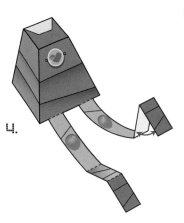

4.

4. Build the body in the same way, gluing tabs 9a–12a to 9b–12b. Fold back the feet at the creases nearest the ends of the legs and glue 13a to 13b, and 14a to 14b.

5. Glue the head to the body, fixing 8a on top of 8b.

6. Attach the arms through the slits of the body.

5.

J-GO the Baby

Baby Nicholas is Nicolo and Angelica Spark's youngest son. They call him J-GO—"J" is for Junior and "GO" is what he loves to do. When he grows up, he wants to be a professional robo racer. For now, he likes playing with his father's inventions though he also enjoys playing tag with the butler.

DIFFICULTY RATING

CONSTRUCTION INSTRUCTIONS

1. Detach the templates from page 89.

2. Prefold all creases marked with a dotted white line.

3. Assemble the baby by gluing tabs 1a–7a under the corresponding edges, then tuck in 8a and 9a to 8b and 9b, respectively.

4. Assemble the cradle, forming a box into which J-Go can slip, by gluing tabs 10a–13a behind edges 10b–13b.

5. Assemble tank tracks by gluing all the remaining tabs to their respective edges.

6. Attach the cradle to the tracks by gluing 28a to 28b and 29a to 29b.

7. Place J-Go inside the cradle.

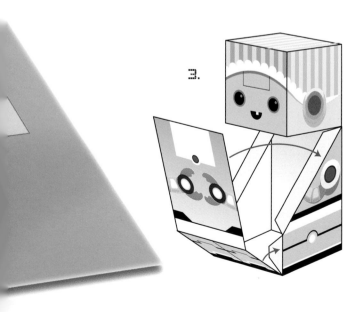

3.

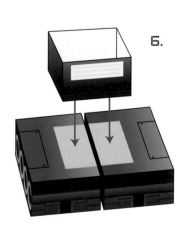

6.

Spinner
the washing machine

The washing machine was one of the professor's first inventions. He thought washing machines should not only be able to wash the dirty laundry but also be able to pick it out from the hamper, dry it, and then return it to the closet. This washing machine comes with 3 spin cycles as well as a great sense of humor.

CONSTRUCTION INSTRUCTIONS

1. Detach the templates from page 91.

2. Prefold all creases, making sure you press out the slits where the arms will go.

3. Assemble the head, gluing tabs 1a–4a underneath their respective edges.

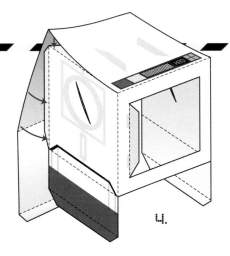

4. Assemble the body, gluing tabs 5a–11a underneath their respective edges.

5. Attach the door to the body, gluing tab 12a to 12b,

6. Attach the head to the body, gluing 13a to 13b.

7. Attach the arms through the slits of the body.

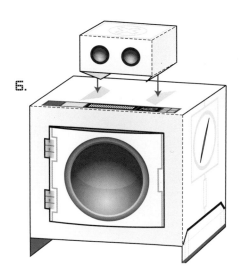

DIFFICULTY
RATING

crunch
the trash compactor

The trash compactor is another one of Professor Spark's inventions. He disliked throwing out the trash after dinner, so he invented the compactor to get rid of it for him. Crunch not only compacts trash for the manor, he also recylces it into new materials that the Professor can use in his inventions.

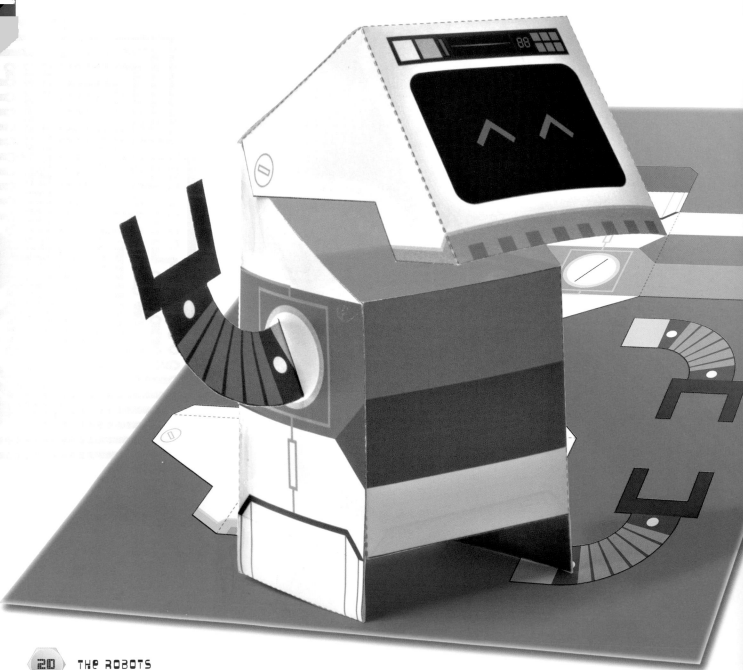

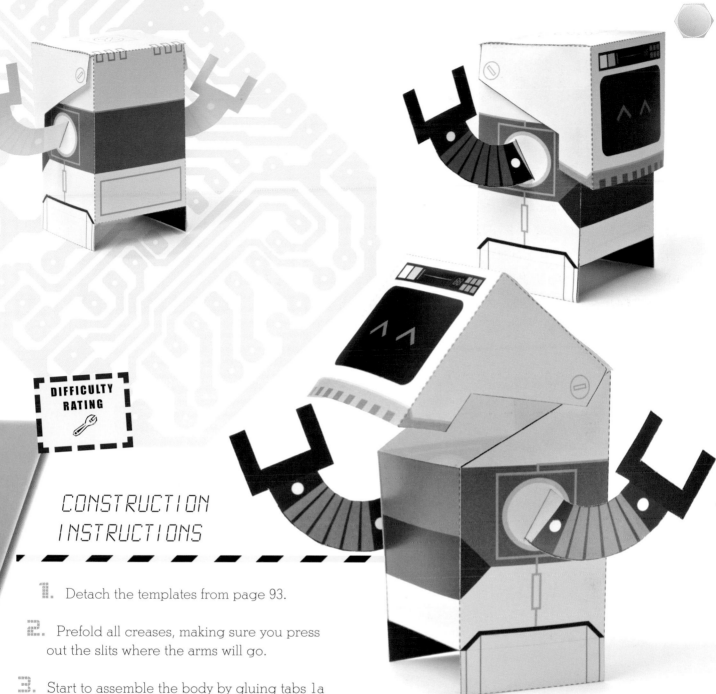

CONSTRUCTION
INSTRUCTIONS

1. Detach the templates from page 93.

2. Prefold all creases, making sure you press out the slits where the arms will go.

3. Start to assemble the body by gluing tabs 1a and 2a under edges 1b and 2b respectively.

4. Fold 3a and 4a back underneath 3b and 4b and glue in place then finish by gluing tabs 5a and 6a underneath edges 5b and 6b.

5. Attach the arms through the slits of the body.

4.

ROBO-EL
the Butler

ROBO-EL is the butler at Spark Manor where he has served the Spark family for generations. Over the years, ROBO-EL has perfected the recipe for very good oiled tea though he also has to play tag with J-GO, the professor's youngest son, which he very much dislikes.

CONSTRUCTION INSTRUCTIONS

1. Detach the templates from page 95, making sure the slit marked across the front of the upper body is pressed out.

2. Prefold all creases marked with a dotted white line.

3. Assemble the upper body, gluing tabs 1a–4a underneath their respective edges.

4. Assemble the lower body, gluing tabs 5a–11a under their respective edges.

5. Stick tabs 12a and 13a on the upper body onto the lower body, aligning them with with points 12b and 13b.

6. Assemble each of the refreshments, gluing tabs 14a–17a under their respective edges.

7. Glue the three refreshments anywhere on the tray, except for the area marked with an X.

8. Slip the tray into the slit in the front part of the upper body.

5.

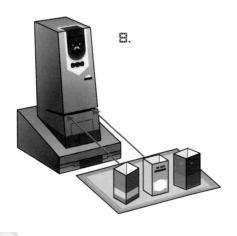

8.

piaget
the painter

piaget is a very talented artist, using his special ink pack to created colorful masterpieces. He has a very successful show in the robot city gallery called "splatworks."

CONSTRUCTION INSTRUCTIONS

1. Detach the templates from page 97.

2. Prefold all creases to make the shape of the robot and prepare them for gluing.

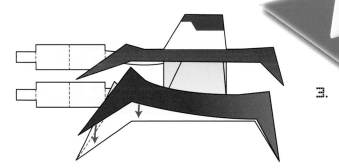

3.

3. Assemble the robot's body, gluing the tabs 1a–10a under their respective edges.

4.

4. Fold up the ink pack, gluing tabs 11a–15a under the corresponding edges and tucking in tabs 16a and 17a without gluing them.

5. Stick the ink pack onto the body, gluing 18a onto 18b on the body.

DIFFICULTY
RATING

RaNdy
the wrestler

RandY is one of robot city's professional wrestlers. He is very competitive and hates losing. Luckily it doesn't happen too often.

DIFFICULTY RATING

CONSTRUCTION INSTRUCTIONS

1. Detach the templates from page 99.

2. Prefold all creases to prepare them for gluing.

3. To assemble the body, first glue tabs 1a–4a under the corresponding edges marked 1b–4b.

4. Next fold the arms and legs in half, turning 5a–8a underneath themselves and gluing them in place.

5. Assemble the head, gluing tabs 9a–12a under their correponding edges marked 9b–12b, and folding up the robot's teeth.

6. Fix the head onto the body, gluing tab 13a on the head onto 13b on the body.

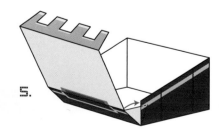

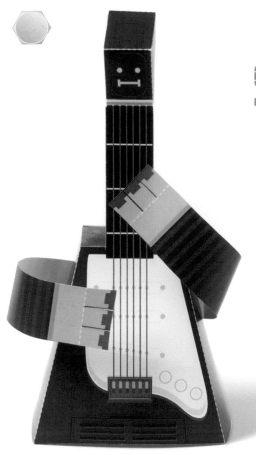

strum
the strings musician

Strum plays the strings in the up-and-coming musical group, The Circuits. He can sound like a guitar, violin, or bass—or else his very own individual sound which is like nothing else in Robot City.

CONSTRUCTION INSTRUCTIONS

1. Detach the templates from page 101, make sure you press out the slits where the arms will go.

2. Prefold all creases to make the robot ready for gluing.

3. Assemble the body by gluing tabs 1a–8a underneath the corresponding parts 1b–8b.

4. Attach the two arms through the slits in the side of the body.

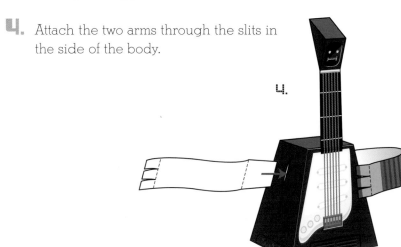

4.

DIFFICULTY
RATING

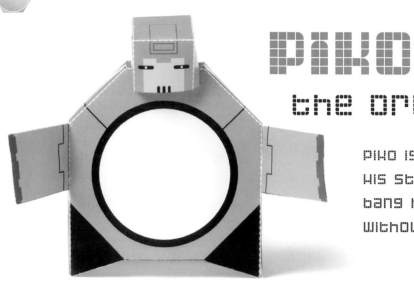

PIKO
the drummer

PIKO is the drummer of the circuits. His strong body ensures he can bang his drums for hours at a time without stopping.

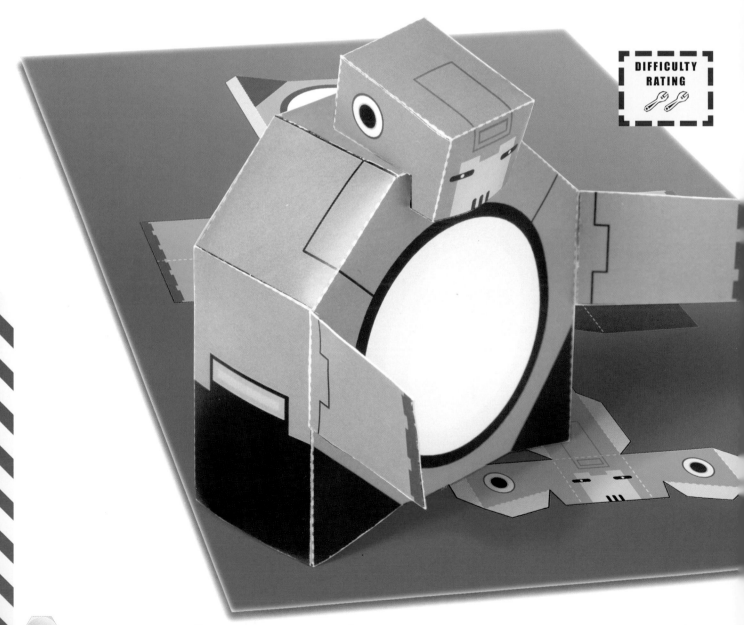

DIFFICULTY RATING

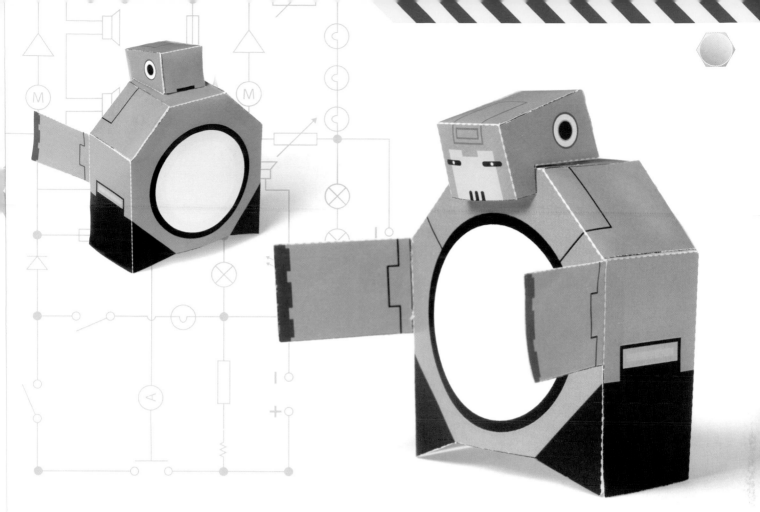

CONSTRUCTION INSTRUCTIONS

1. Detach the templates from page 103.

2. Prefold all creases so that they are ready to be bent and stuck to form the robot.

3. Assemble the body by gluing tabs 1a–10a underneath the corresponding parts 1b–10b.

4. Assemble the head by gluing tabs 11a–14a underneath the corresponding parts 11b–14b.

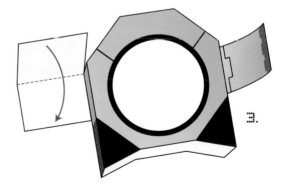

5. Attach the head to the body by gluing flaps 15a and 16a on the head onto parts 15b and 16b on the body.

FELINUS

the cat

FELINUS WAS ROBO-EL'S SUGGESTION. HE WAS TIRED OF WASTING TIME BEING CHASED AROUND THE MANOR BY J-GO AND DOUG THE DOG SO HE ASKED THE PROFESSOR TO INVENT THE CAT TO TAKE HIS PLACE. ROBO-EL IS NOW HAPPY GOING ABOUT HIS TASKS IN THE MANOR.

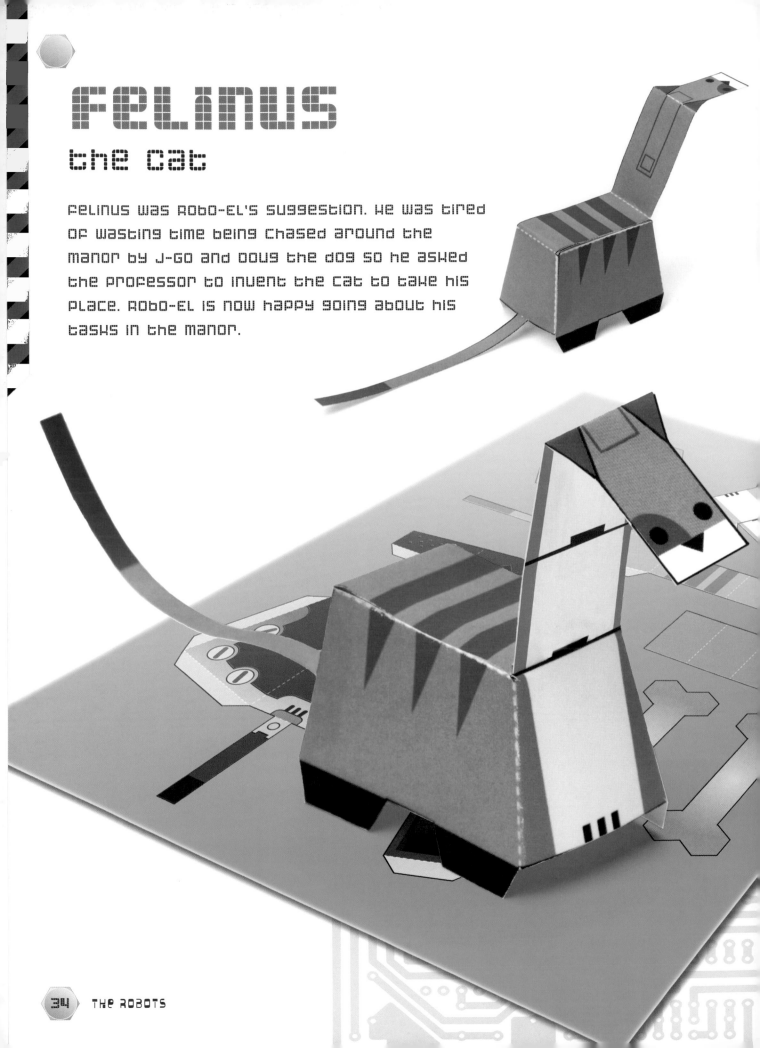

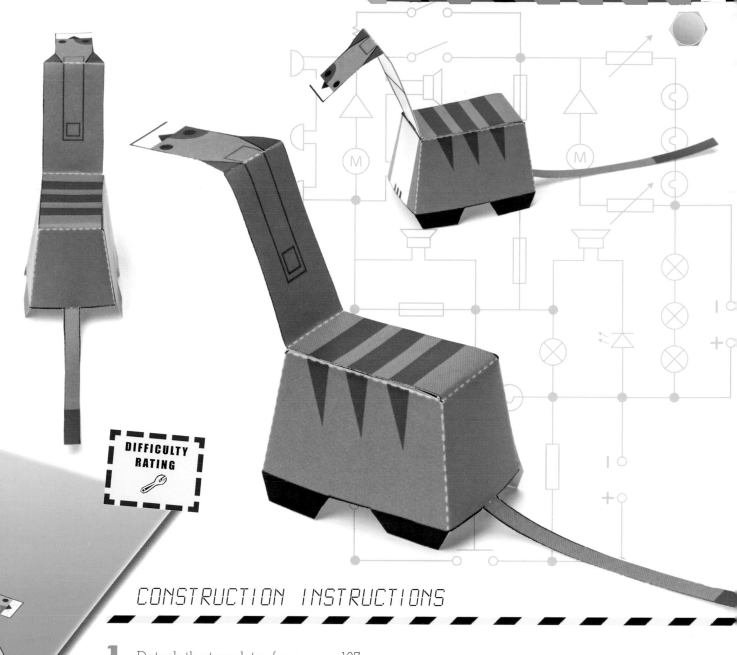

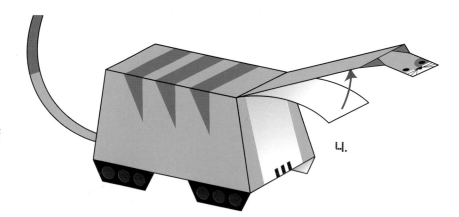

CONSTRUCTION INSTRUCTIONS

1. Detach the templates from page 107.

2. Prefold all creases in preparation for making up the robot.

3. Assemble the cat, gluing tabs 1a–3a under the edges marked 1b–3b.

4. Glue 4a under 4b to make the underside of the cat's neck.

DIFFICULTY RATING

4.

DOUG

the DOG

When J-GO was born, his mother thought it would be a great idea for him to have a playmate so Prof. Spark created Doug to be J-GO's loyal and lifelong companion—they've been inseparable ever since. Doug loves to sniff and fetch.

CONSTRUCTION INSTRUCTIONS

1. Detach the templates from page 107.

2. Prefold all creases in preparation for making up the robot and dog toy.

3. Assemble the robot dog by gluing the tabs 1a–8a underneath edges 1b–8b respectively.

4. Assemble the dog toy by making a square tube, and use the bone and food bowl as objects for Doug to sniff.

DIFFICULTY RATING

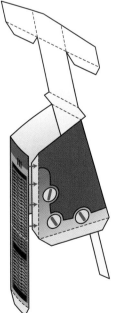

3.

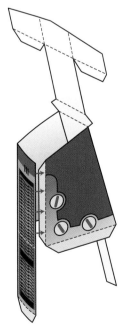

Shelley
the Turtle

Shelley is J-Go's swimming instructor. J-Go was inspired to learn how to swim ever since he saw the professor busily working on his top-secret military whale project.

CONSTRUCTION INSTRUCTIONS

DIFFICULTY RATING

1. Detach the template from page 109.

2. Prefold all creases in preparation for making up the robot.

3. Assemble the turtle by gluing tabs 1a–8a, in order, to the edges marked 1b–8b.

4. Curl the legs upwards in the middle so that they resemble the ones in the photograph by running a pencil along the underside of each one.

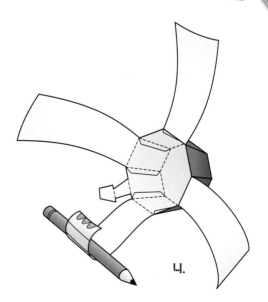

4.

mobius
the whale

We don't have that much information about this invention. All we know is that Professor Spark developed it for the military and it remains top secret—though it must be a special robot designed to help fight Robot City's evil villains.

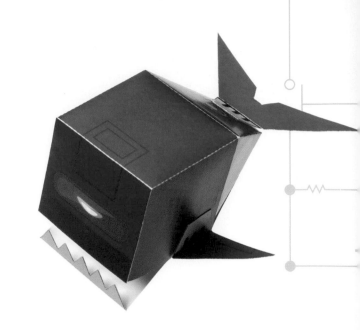

CONSTRUCTION INSTRUCTIONS

1. Detach the templates from page 111.

2. Prefold all creases in preparation for making up the robot.

3. Assemble the body, gluing tabs 1a–8a underneath edges 1b–8b. Ensure the mouth remains open and bend up the teeth at right angles.

3.

4. Attach the fins and tail to the body, gluing edges 9a–11a to 9b–11b.

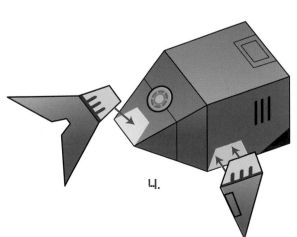

4.

WINGS
the Bird

The bird is actually an aerial camera that sends video footage to the manor's main computer. NICOLO invented the bird to track J-GO and DOUG in their misadventures just so that he knows where they are at all times.

DIFFICULTY RATING

CONSTRUCTION INSTRUCTIONS

1. Detach the templates from page 113.

2. Prefold all creases and make sure you press out the slits where the wings will go.

3. Assemble the beak by gluing tab 1a under edge 1b.

4. Form the robot's body by gluing tabs 2a–6a, in order, underneath their respective edges, 2b–6b.

5. Attach the beak to the body, gluing the two together at 7a and 7b.

6. Attach the wings through the slits in the side of the body.

5 & 6.

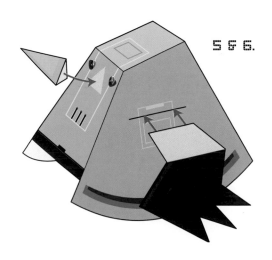

DOCTOR SOCKET
the Repair Doctor

Robot City has many citizens, and they all have to be in tip-top shape. That is the doctor's primary mission and he's kept very busy dealing with all sorts of ailments that affect the city's residents. Whether a robot has rusted joints or needs some internal rewiring, Dr Socket has the know-how to make everyone right as rain.

DIFFICULTY RATING

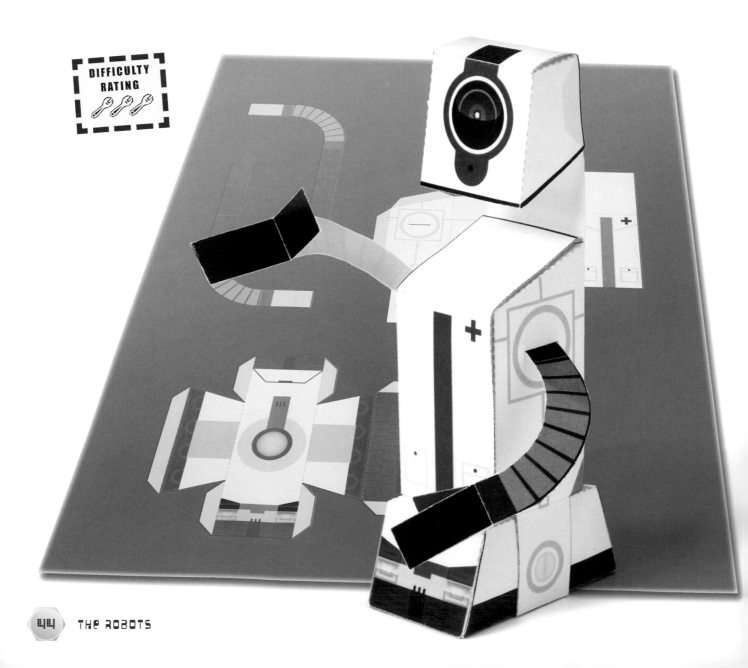

CONSTRUCTION INSTRUCTIONS

1. Detach the templates from page 115.

2. Prefold all creases and make sure you press out the slits where the arms will go.

3. Start to assemble the body by gluing tabs 1a–5a in order underneath the edges marked 1b–5b.

4. Fold down flap marked 6a and glue it in place against the two flaps marked 6b.

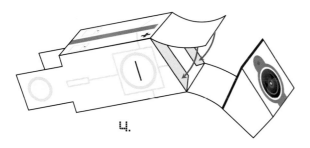

4.

5. Assemble the tracked base by gluing tabs 7a–13a to the underside of the edges marked 7b–13b.

6. Connect the two parts by sliding the body over the tracked base and gluing tabs 14b and 15b to parts 14a and 15a.

7. Attach the arms through the slits in the side of the body.

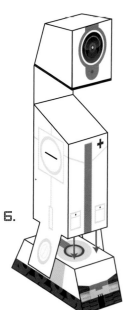

6.

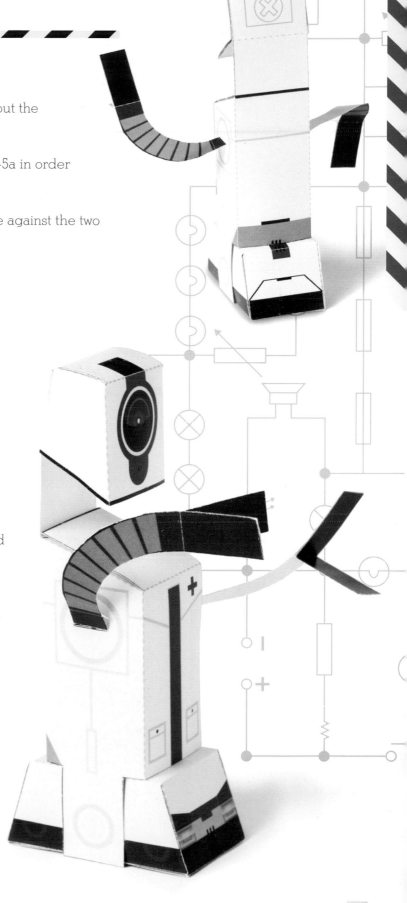

A.R.P.
the AUtomated Repair Platform

AN ARP IS a patient's personal robotics physician. The patient lies on the ARP to be monitored and repaired based on the doctor's diagnosis. Every ARP comes with a mini droid that shuttles supplies back and forth.

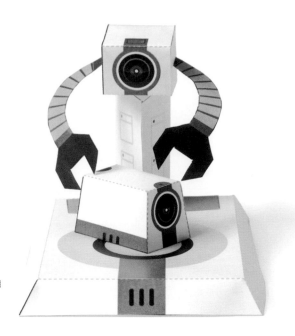

CONSTRUCTION INSTRUCTIONS

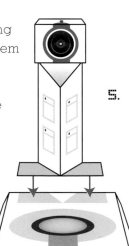

1. Detach the templates from page 117.

2. Prefold all creases, making sure you press out the slits where the arms will go.

3. Assemble the body by gluing tabs 1a–6a behind the edges marke 1b–6b respectively.

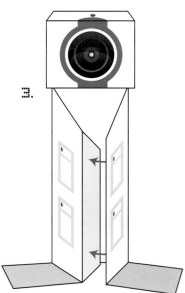

4. Assemble the platform, gluing tabs 7a–10a behind the edges marked 7b–10b.

5. Stick the body to the platform by folding back flaps 11a and 12a then sticking them with glue to areas 11b and 12b.

6. Attach the arms through the slits in the side of the head.

7. Assemble the Lab Assistant by gluing tabs 13a–16a under the edge marked 13b–16b.

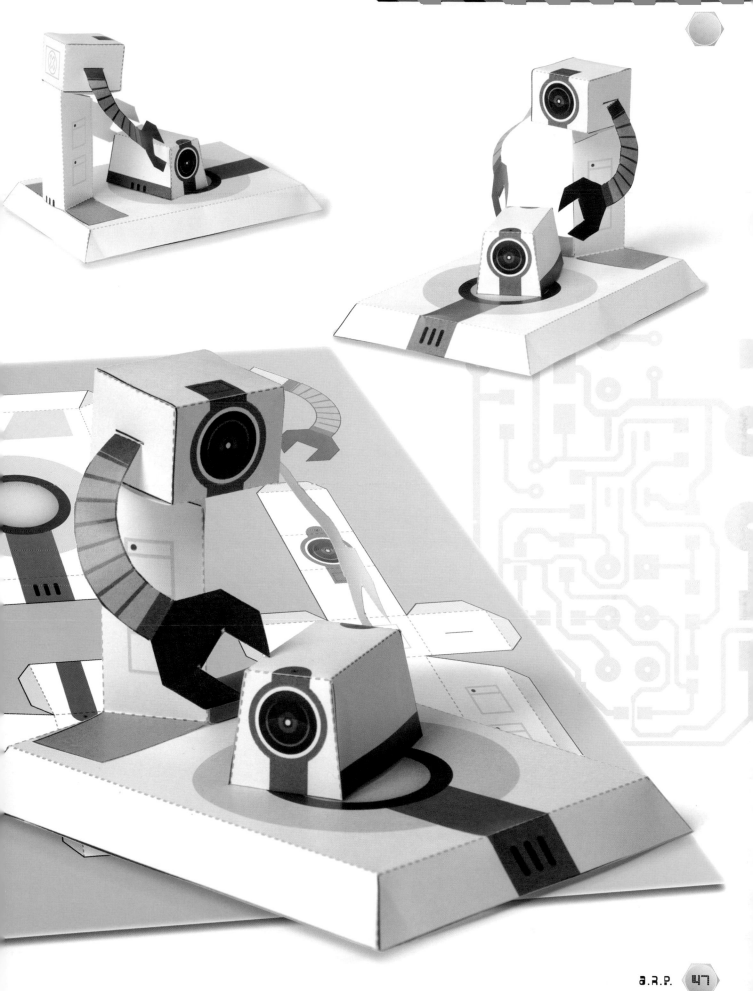

NURSE C09
the Repair Nurse

Nurse C09 assists the doctor in all of his operations. She graduated first in her class from robo medical school and has been working with Dr Socket for the last year. She loves her work and her bedside manner is a hit with the 'bots she looks after.

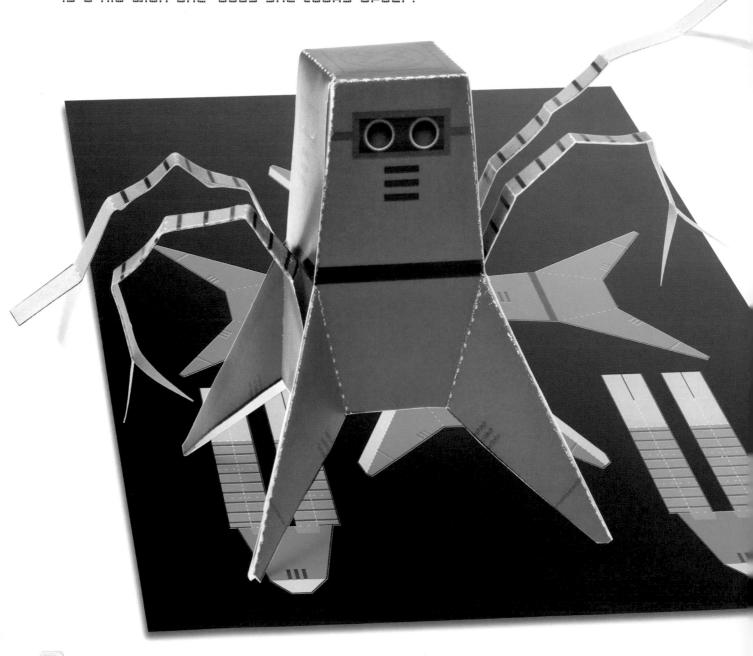

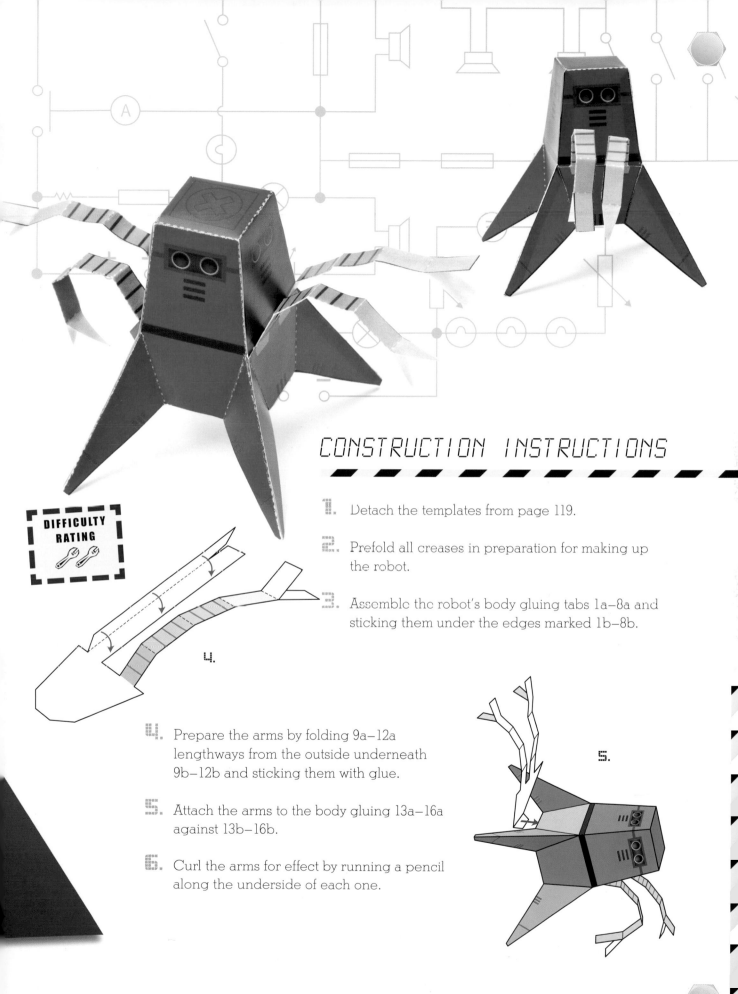

CONSTRUCTION INSTRUCTIONS

DIFFICULTY RATING

1. Detach the templates from page 119.

2. Prefold all creases in preparation for making up the robot.

3. Assemble the robot's body gluing tabs 1a–8a and sticking them under the edges marked 1b–8b.

4. Prepare the arms by folding 9a–12a lengthways from the outside underneath 9b–12b and sticking them with glue.

5. Attach the arms to the body gluing 13a–16a against 13b–16b.

6. Curl the arms for effect by running a pencil along the underside of each one.

4.

5.

BOB the SICK ROBOT

THIS IS BOB, HE HAS TUMMY PROBLEMS WHICH HAVE CAUSED ALL SORTS OF ISSUES WHILE HE'S AT WORK AT THE LOCAL RESTAURANT. HIS INTERNAL CIRCUITS HAVE BEEN FRIED BECAUSE OF HIS LOVE OF EXTRA-SPICY CHILI OIL, AND HE'S IN DESPERATE NEED OF AN OVERHAUL FROM THE DOCTOR. IT'S NOTHING A FEW NEW BOLTS WON'T FIX, SO HE'LL SOON BE SMILING AGAIN.

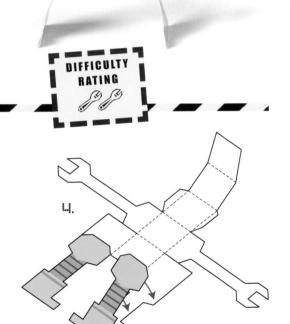

CONSTRUCTION INSTRUCTIONS

DIFFICULTY RATING

1. Detach the templates from page 121.

2. Prefold all creases in preparation for making up the robot.

3. Assemble the head by gluing tabs 1a–4a behind the edges marked 1b–4b then fold over the flap marked 5a without sticking so that it can be lifted up.

4. Start forming the body by folding up flaps 6a and 7a and gluing them in place against 6b and 7b to form the legs.

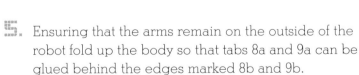

5. Ensuring that the arms remain on the outside of the robot fold up the body so that tabs 8a and 9a can be glued behind the edges marked 8b and 9b.

6. Finish the body by folding up tab 10a so that it sits against flap 10b but do not glue it in position.

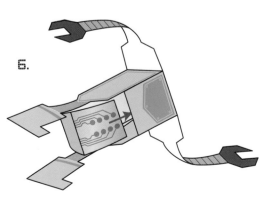

7. Attach the head to the body by sticking together 11a and 11b.

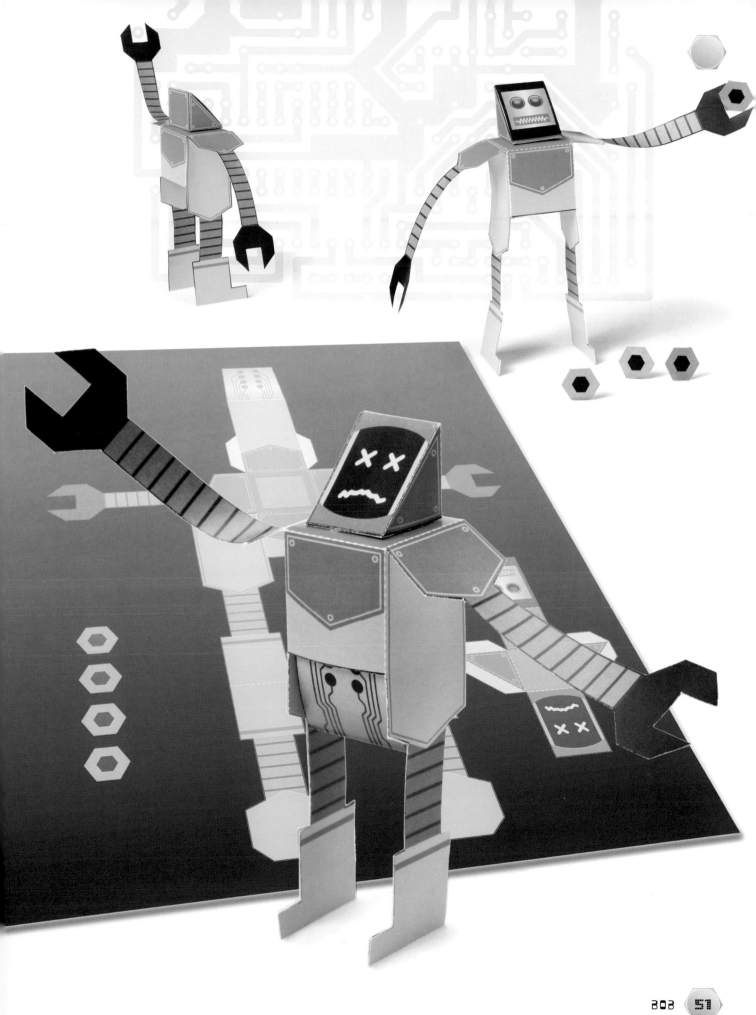

MR Gibbs
the mayor

The mayor is a "get things done" type of robot. As he runs Robot City all on his own he has become very good at multi-tasking—his four arms help a lot.

CONSTRUCTION INSTRUCTIONS

DIFFICULTY RATING

1. Detach the templates from page 123, making sure you press out the slits where the arms will go.

2. Fold and release all the creases so they are ready for gluing.

3. Assemble the body gluing the tabs marked 1a–12a underneath the corresponding parts 1b–12b.

4. Attach the four arms through the slits in the side of the body.

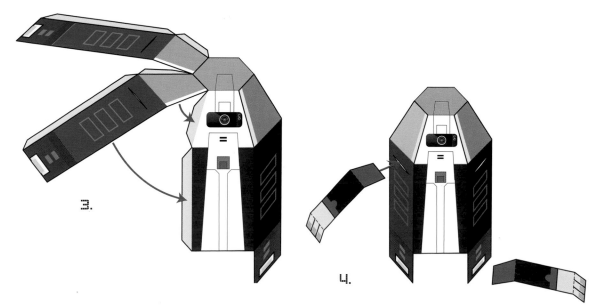

3.

4.

Captain BLUE

the eye in the sky

The Captain is Robot City's head of security. He leads a task force of sentries and scouts and is always ready to deal with danger—anytime, anywhere. If necessary, the Captain will combine with sentry units for extra firepower and armor.

CONSTRUCTION INSTRUCTIONS

DIFFICULTY RATING

1. Detach the templates from page 125.

2. Prefold all creases and press out the slits into which the arms will slide.

3. Make up the body, folding back parts 1a and 2a and sticking in place, then gluing tabs 3a–8a beneath their corresponding edges.

4. Assemble the arms by folding part 9a back behind 9b and gluing, then turning 10a over and gluing to 10b, Repeat on the other arm with parts 11 and 12.

5. Attach the arms through the slits in the sides of the body.

6. To give him even greater powers, attach Captain Blue to the Sentry Unit on page 57.

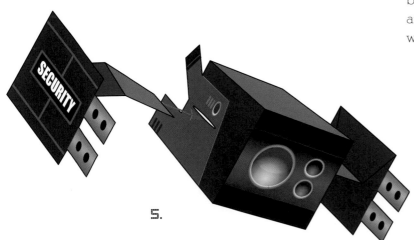

5.

SCOUT UNIT
SECURITY SCOUT

NUMEROUS SCOUT UNITS HAVE BEEN DEPLOYED AROUND ROBOT CITY TO FUNCTION AS INVESTIGATORY UNITS, GATHERING INFORMATION AND INTELLIGENCE. THESE FAST AND AGILE UNITS ARE VERY IMPORTANT MEMBERS OF THE SECURITY TEAM.

CONSTRUCTION INSTRUCTIONS

DIFFICULTY RATING

1. Detach the templates from page 127.

2. Prefold all creases marked with a dotted white line.

3. Assemble the base, gluing tabs 1a–4a to their corresponding edges.

4. Assemble the legs by folding each element in half. Fold back the square ends 9a–16a then glue 5a–8a to 5b–8b. Take care not to glue the ends 9a–16a now.

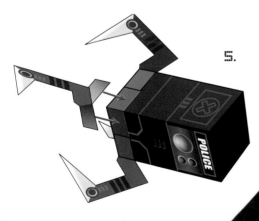

5.

5. Glue the legs to the body by adding glue to 9a–16a and attaching to 9b–16b.

sentry unit

security sentry

sentry units were designed to be watchdogs that patrol the city to keep it safe and secure. with its mounted rocket launchers, it is the security team's main source of firepower. each sentry unit can combine with the captain to increase its hand-to-hand capabilities and upgrade its tactical battle computer.

DIFFICULTY RATING

CONSTRUCTION INSTRUCTIONS

1. Detach the templates from page 127.

2. Prefold all creases marked with a dotted white line.

3. Assemble the body, gluing tabs 1a–3a to their corresponding edges and tucking 4a some of the way into the gap left at 4b to show the missile launchers.

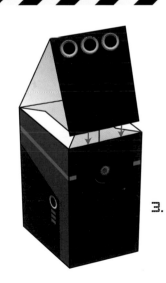

3.

4. Assemble the tank tracks by gluing tabs 5a–9a behind 5b–9b and 10a–14a behind 10b–14b.

5. Attach the body to the tracks by joining points 15a–16a to 15b–16b.

ultrabot
the hero

When the going gets tough, the tough call ultrabot, Robot City's very own high-flying superhero. He has missiles and lasers to deal with threats as well as his three sidekicks—Ariel, Lando, and Cecile—who help him deal with the villains of the city.

DIFFICULTY RATING

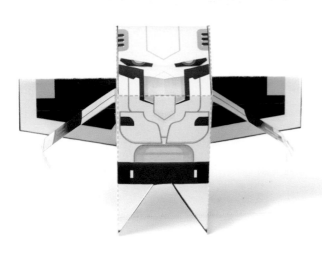

CONSTRUCTION INSTRUCTIONS

1. Detach the templates from page 129.

2. Prefold all creases and make sure you press out the slits where the arms will go.

3. Assemble the body, gluing tabs 1a–6a under their respective edges.

4. Assemble the wing pack by folding it in half and gluing 7a to 7b.

5. Attach the wing pack to the body, gluing 8a to 8b.

6. Attach the arms through the slits in the side of the body, choosing whichever pair you think works best.

5

DR YUELL

the villainous mastermind

YUELL IS ULTRABOT'S NEMESIS. NOT MUCH IS KNOWN OF THIS EVIL MASTERMIND—NO-ONE EVEN KNOWS HIS TRUE NAME. BUT EVERYONE IN ROBOT CITY HAS EXPERIENCED HIS MONSTROUS HANDIWORK AND IS ON GUARD AGAINST HIS EVIL INTENTIONS.

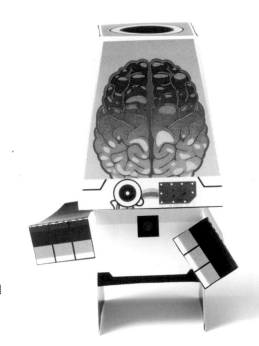

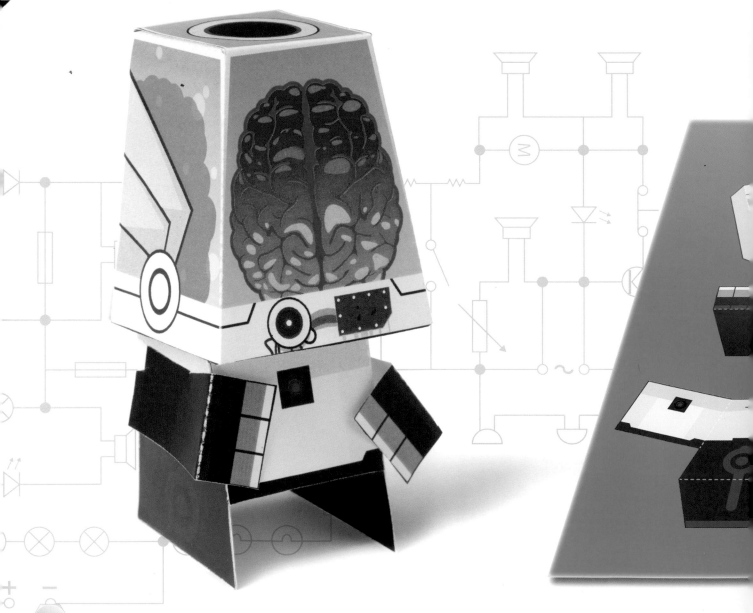

CONSTRUCTION INSTRUCTIONS

1. Detach the templates from page 129.

2. Prefold all creases, making sure you press out the slits in the body where the arms will go.

3. Start assembling the robot by gluing tabs 1a–4a behind the edges marked 1b–4b, forming the head.

4. Turn back flaps 5a and 6a, gluing them in place against edges 5b and 6b, forming the legs.

5. Form the robot's body by gluing tab 7a behind the edge marked 7b.

6. Attach the arms through the slits in the side of the body.

5.

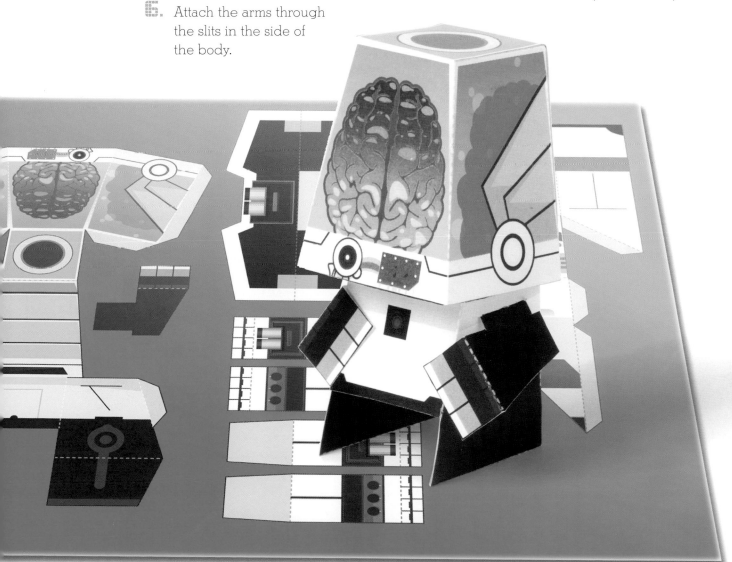

IGOR
the VILLAINOUS BODYGUARD

Every evil genius must have a loyal minion. Igor has served his master, Dr Yuell, for as long as anyone can remember. Igor is very strong and is heavily armored. Wherever Dr Yuell is, Igor will not be far away.

DIFFICULTY RATING

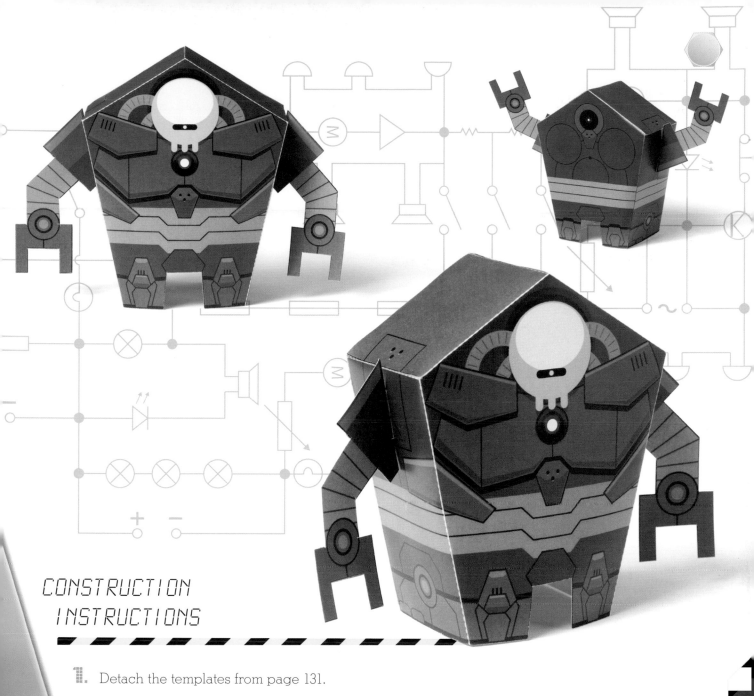

CONSTRUCTION INSTRUCTIONS

1. Detach the templates from page 131.

2. Prefold all creases, making sure you press out the slits where the arms will go.

3. Assemble the body by gluing tabs 1a–6a in sequence behind the edges marked 1b–6b.

4. Attach the arms through the slits in the side of the body.

3.

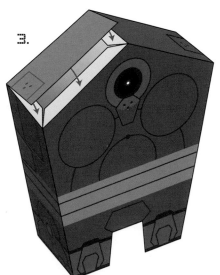

FrankenBot
the Monster

This is the first of Dr Yuell's monstrous creations. He formed the Frankenbot by combining different parts from other robots to make his own terrifying creation.

CONSTRUCTION INSTRUCTIONS

DIFFICULTY RATING

1. Detach the template from page 133.

2. Prefold all creases marked with a dotted white line in preparation for making the robots.

3. Start assembling the body by making the arms and legs, folding 1a–4a underneath themselves and sticking in place with glue.

4. Form the body of the robot by gluing tabs 5a–8a underneath edges 5b–8b.

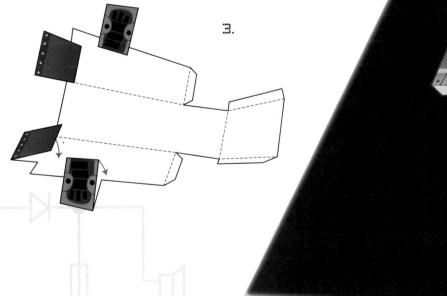

3.

ROBOZILLA
the monster lizard

Dr Yuell invented a gigantification ray and used it on one of his robot lizards. It resulted in a giant mechanized lizard that went on a rampage in Robot City. Luckily, Ultrabot and his sidekicks were around to save the day.

CONSTRUCTION INSTRUCTIONS

DIFFICULTY RATING

1. Detach the templates from page 135.

2. Prefold all creases in preparation for forming the robot.

3. Start assembling the body by folding 1a and 2a back on themselves and gluing in place against 1b and 2b, respectively.

4. Glue tabs 3a–7a behind their respective edges, marked 3b–7b.

5. Attach the tail to the body, gluing 9a to 9b.

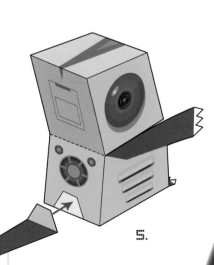

5.

ROBOZILLA

ROBORILLA
the monster gorilla

The ROBORILLA was created by Professor Spark
to counteract the ROBOZILLA menace. It was
designed to have the abilities and strengths of
a gorilla. After the detonation of the
Professor's shrink bomb during its battle with
Robozilla, the ROBORILLA disappeared and its current
location is unknown.

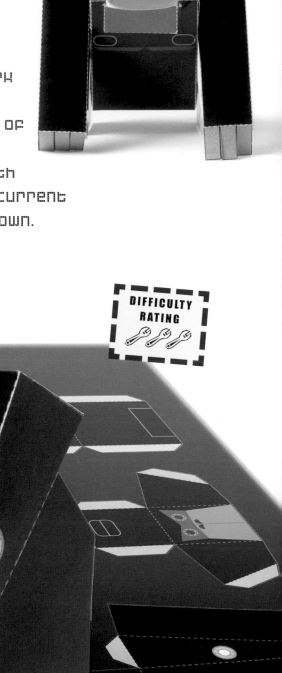

DIFFICULTY
RATING

CONSTRUCTION INSTRUCTIONS

1. Detach the four templates from page 137.

2. Prefold all creases marked with a dotted white line and ensure the slits that make the fingers are open.

3. Assemble the head by gluing tabs 1a–6a underneath the edges marked 1b–6b.

4. Assemble the body by gluing tabs 7a–13a to the relevant edges.

4.

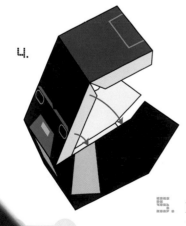

5.

5. Make up the arms, gluing tabs 14a–17a under their respective edges and repeating with tabs 18a–21a.

6. Attach the head to the body, gluing 22a to 22b, and the arms to the body at points 23 and 24.

SIEGE HORSE

the mechanical seahorse

The Siege Horse is a submersible robotic creature that strikes terror in the oily seas around Robot City. It is not known where the seahorse came from or why it appeared. Rest-assured, Ultrabot is ready for the time when it shows up again.

CONSTRUCTION INSTRUCTIONS

DIFFICULTY RATING

1. Detach the template from page 139.

2. Prefold all creases in preparation for forming the shape of the robot.

3. Create the body by gluing tabs 1a–3a behind the edges marked 1b–3b then sticking together 4a and 4b to form the rotary saw.

4. Form the fins by gluing together 5a–7a with 5b–7b.

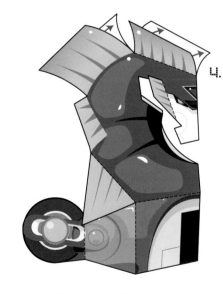

4.

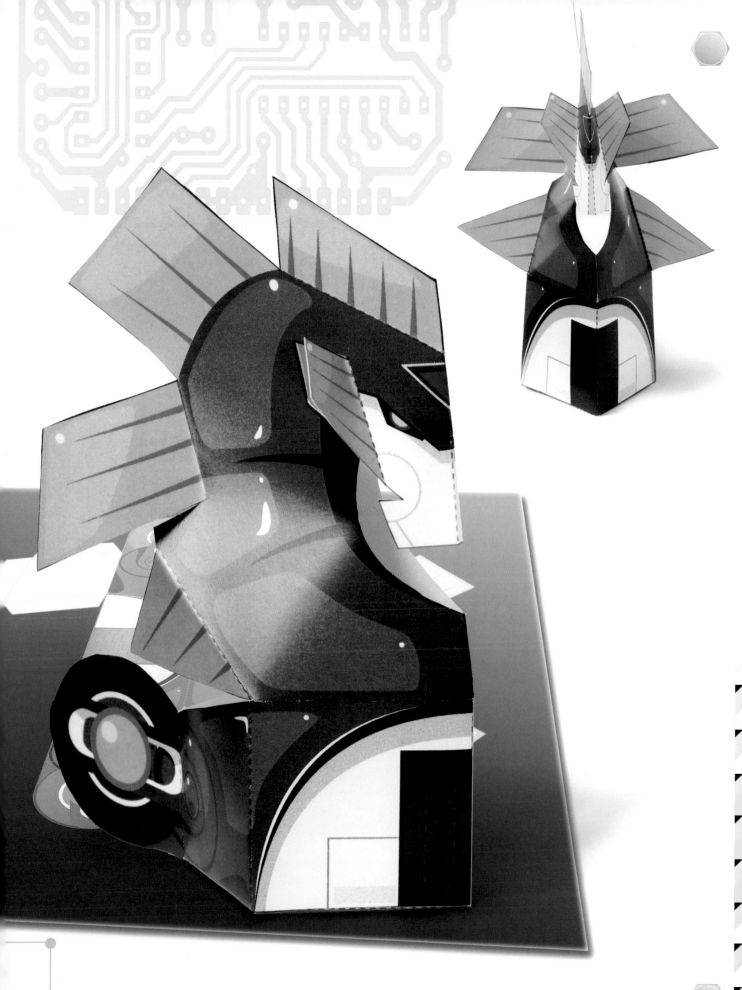

SCORPION LOBSTER
the underwater monster

The scorpion lobster is a monstrosity that combines a scorpion robot's sting with a lobster robot's pincer grip and body armor. This is Dr Yuell's most dangerous creation yet.

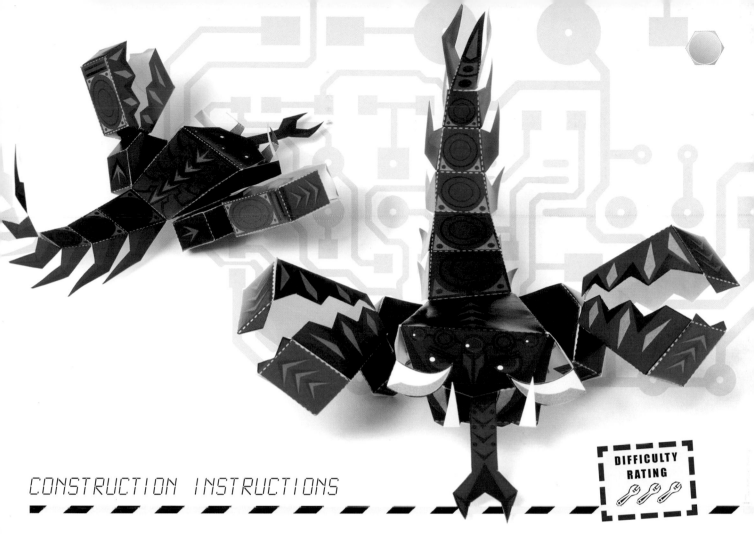

CONSTRUCTION INSTRUCTIONS

1. Detach the templates from page 141.

2. Prefold all creases in preparation for forming the shape of the robot.

3. Attach the tongue by gluing tab 1a onto part 1b.

4. Assemble the body, gluing tab 1c under flap 1d, tab 4c against flap 4b and tab 2c against flap 2b.

5. Assemble the tracks, gluing both tabs 6a under flaps 6b, both tabs 6c under flaps 6d, both tabs 7a under flaps 7b, and both tabs 7c under flaps 7d.

6. Assemble the claws by gluing all tabs 9a and 10a under respective flaps 9b and 10b, then all tabs 9c and 10c under flaps 9d and 10d.

7. Attach the claws to the wheels and then the wheels to the body, gluing panels 8a and 11a to tabs 8b and 11b. Finish by gluing 3a and 5a under 3b and 5b respectively then sticking 4b to 4a and 2b to 2a.

DIFFICULTY RATING

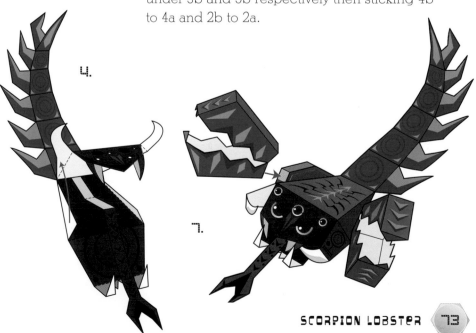

4.

7.

The SideKicks

Ariel, Lando, and Cecile are Ultrabot's sidekicks. Each robot has a different specialization.

SideKick Lando

Lando moves on a single track, is very strong, and can lift 10 times his own weight—he is also an expert boxer.

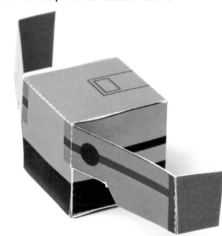

CONSTRUCTION INSTRUCTIONS

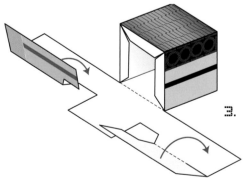

3.

DIFFICULTY RATING

1   Detach the three templates from page 143.

2   Prefold all creases marked with a dotted white line in preparation for making the robots.

3   Assemble Lando, the tracked sidekick, by gluing tabs 1a–7a under their resective edges.

4   Fold 8a and 9a underneath 8b and 9b repectively, ensuring the slits have been opened out alongside the track, and glue in place.

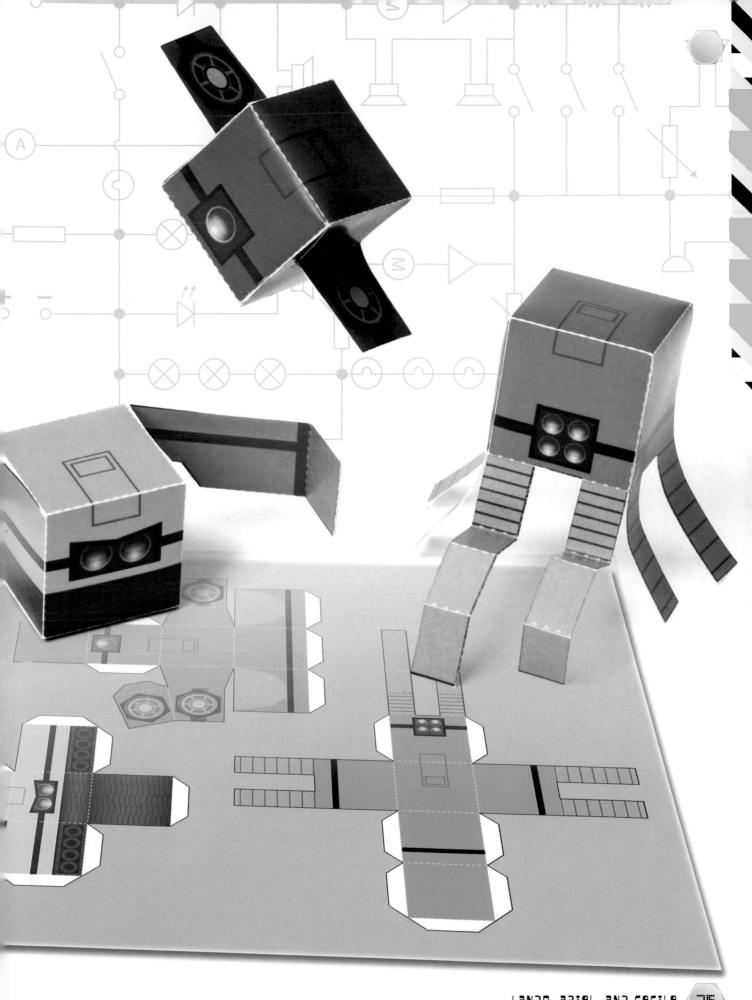

SIDEKICK ARIEL

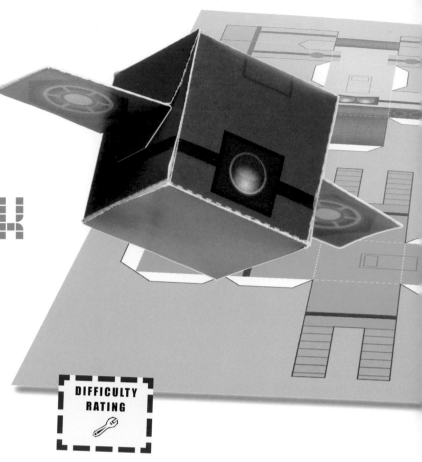

Ariel has flight capability—he specializes in information gathering, sniping, and aerial acrobatics.

DIFFICULTY RATING

CONSTRUCTION INSTRUCTIONS

1. Assemble Ariel by gluing tabs 1a–5a under 1b–5b.

2. Fold 6a under 6b to make a wing and glue in place. Fold down 7a and stick against 7b, repeating for tabs 8a and 8b.

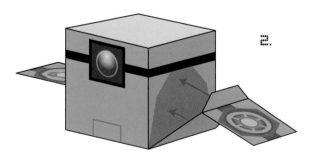

3. Repeat the previous step on the other side of the model for points 9, 10, and 11.

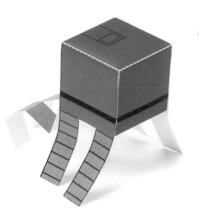

SideKICK CeCILE

Cecile is an expert in underwater operations, demolitions, and wrestling.

CONSTRUCTION INSTRUCTIONS

DIFFICULTY RATING

1. Assemble Cecile, gluing tabs 1a–7a underneath points 1b–7b.

2. Form Cecile's pincers by folding in half at points 8a and 9a and stiking with glue to 8b and 9b.

3. Assemble the tentacles, twist each one for effect.

3.

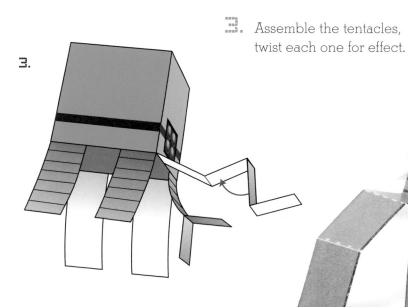

index

Note: Bold page numbers refer
to Templates

acknowledgments

Thanks to Thomas Hamlyn-Harris for paper toy and book-related guidance.

Thanks to Ron Rementilla, the creator of www.paperkraft.net, for continuously featuring all the creative and inspiring paper toys from around the world.

Thanks to Brian Castleforte for putting up www.nicepapertoys.com, which I'd say is the official online home of paper toy artists of all ages.

Thanks to Marc Aldrin Collado and Carl Zeno Manalo for helping me with the toy textures and templates found in this book.

Thanks to Pete Jorgensen and the CICO team for publishing this book with me. Your patience and guidance as we went through the production process was very much appreciated.

Thanks to everyone who has visited www.papertoyadventures.com and who I've had the pleasure of interacting with through it.

Many, many, many thanks to all the creative people out there for all of your inspiring works of art.

And finally, thanks to my family, who has always been very supportive of my projects, however crazy they are.

The publisher would like to thank Galina Zapletnuka for all her help assembling the models.

The Templates

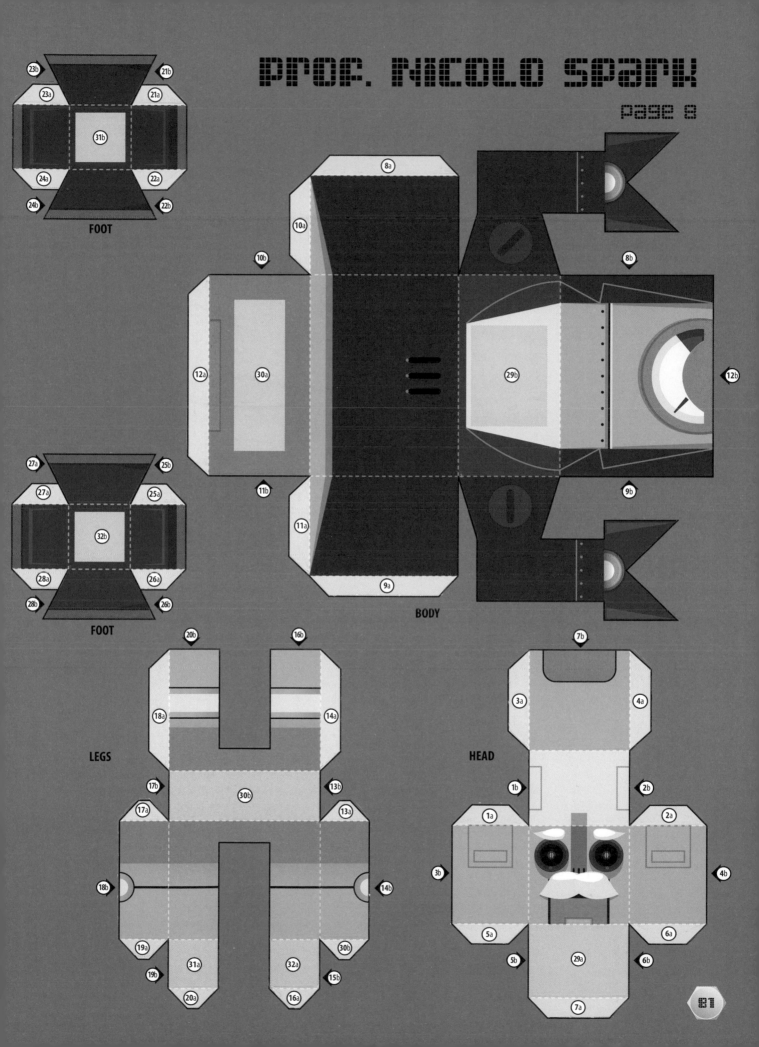

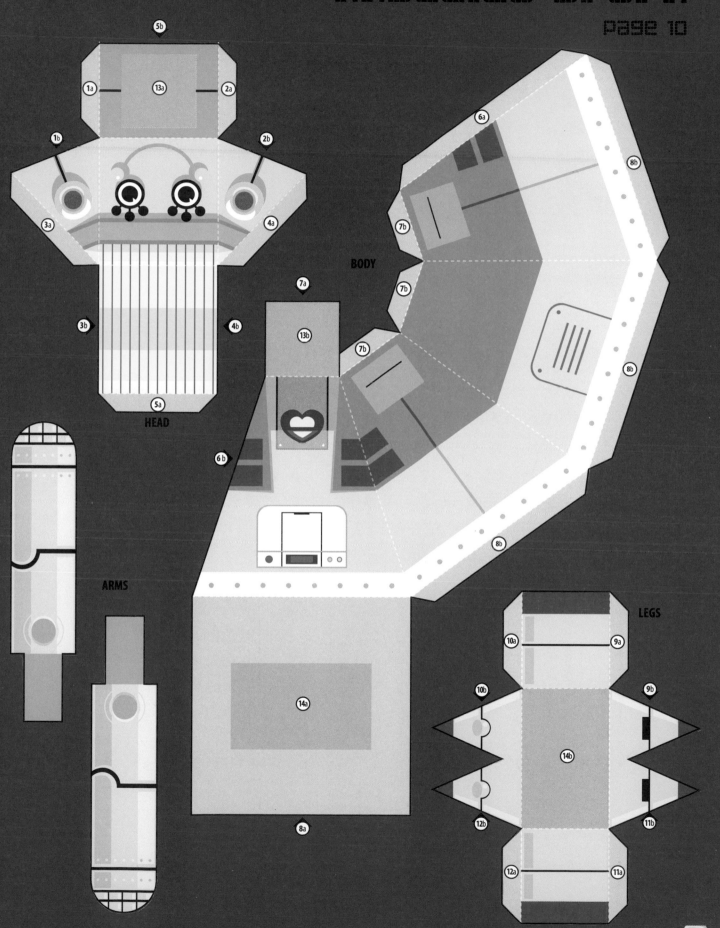

HEAD

BODY

ARMS

LEGS

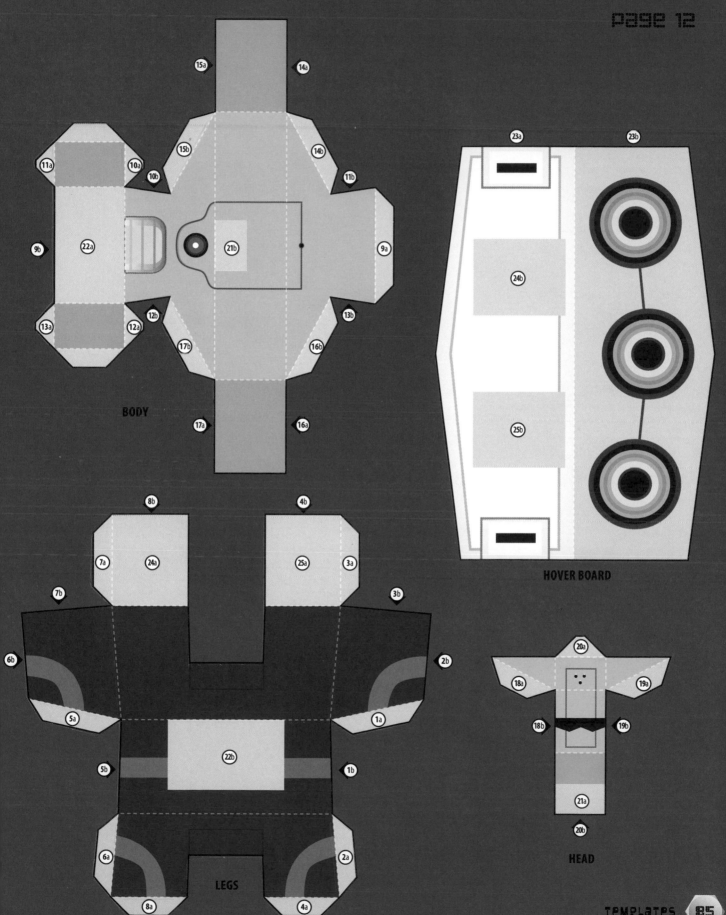

BODY

HOVER BOARD

LEGS

HEAD

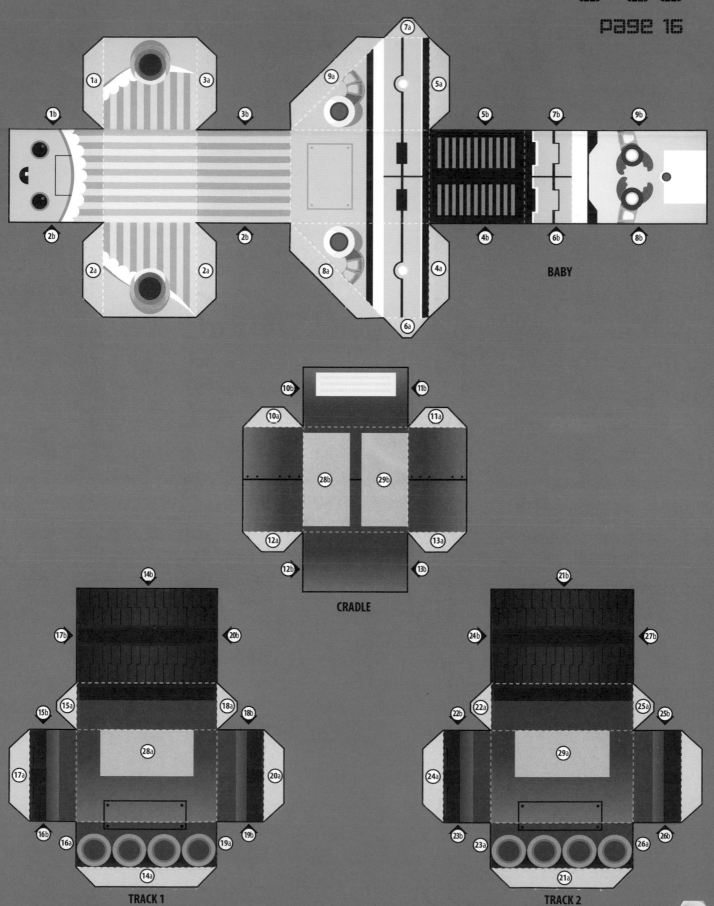

BABY

CRADLE

TRACK 1

TRACK 2

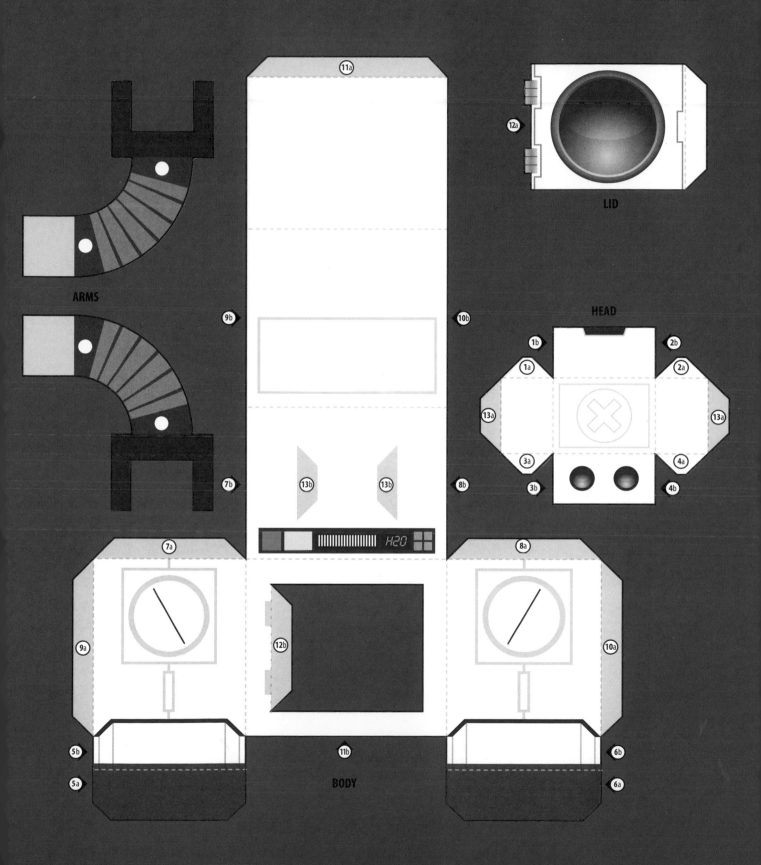

LID

ARMS

HEAD

H2O

BODY

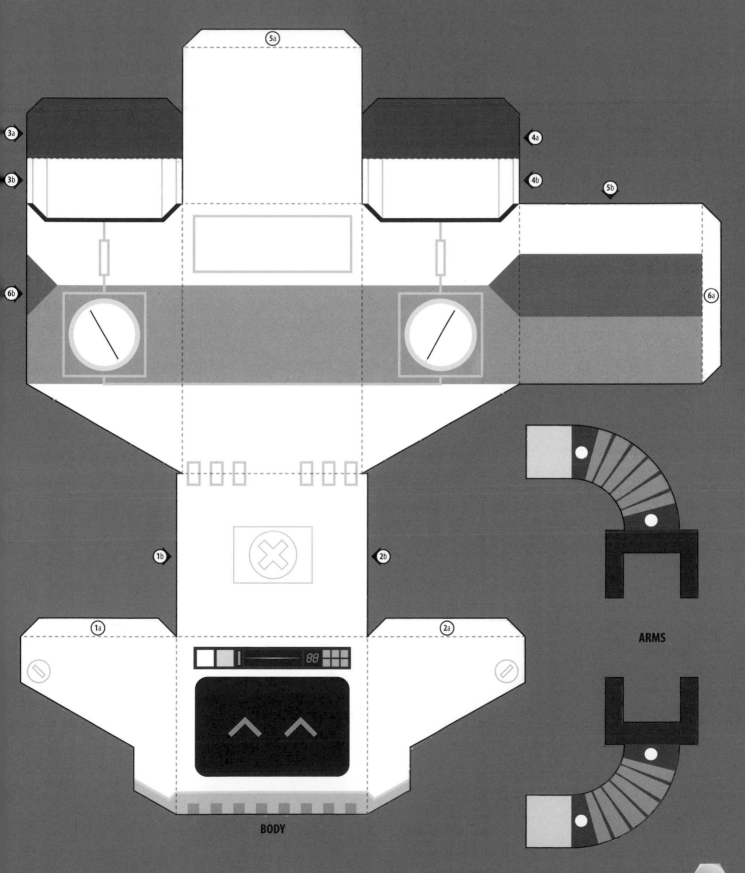

ARMS

BODY

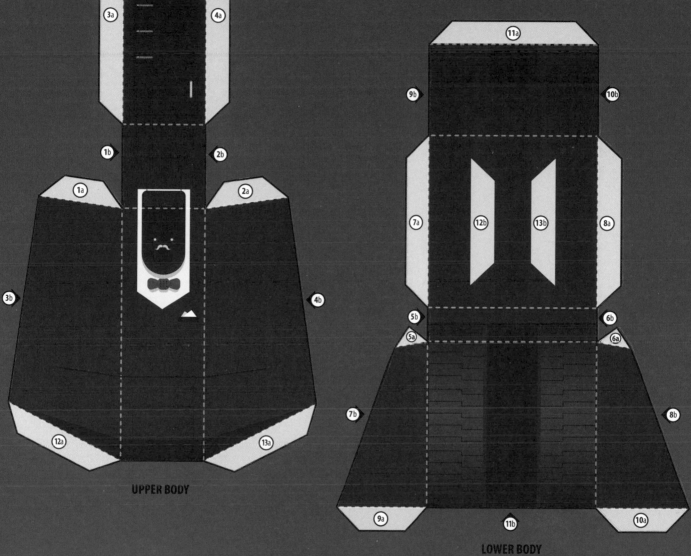

UPPER BODY

LOWER BODY

TRAY

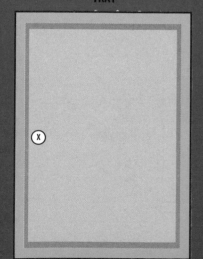

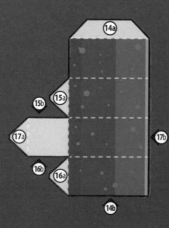

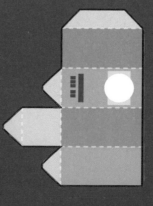

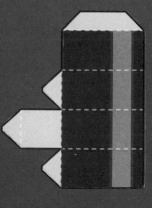

REFRESHMENTS

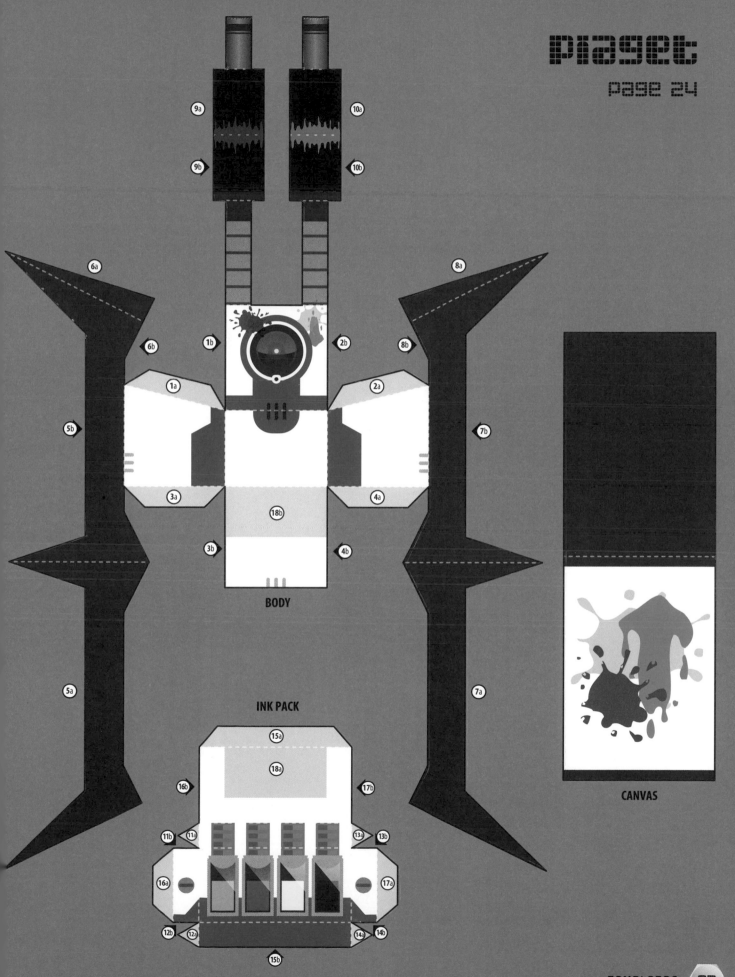

BODY

INK PACK

CANVAS

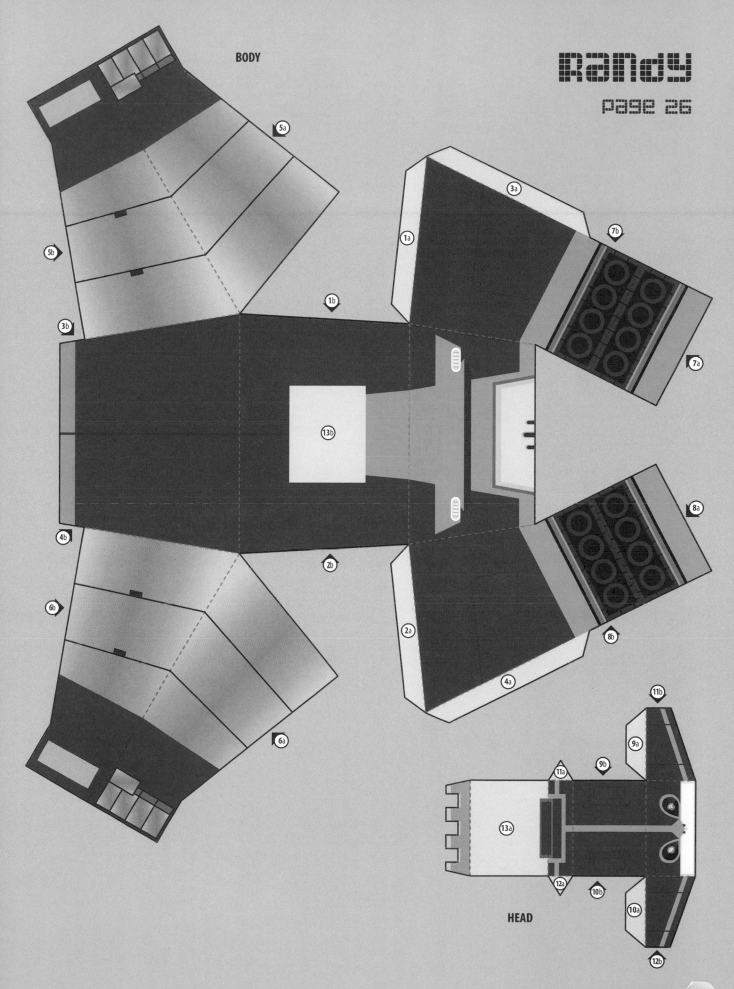

BODY

HEAD

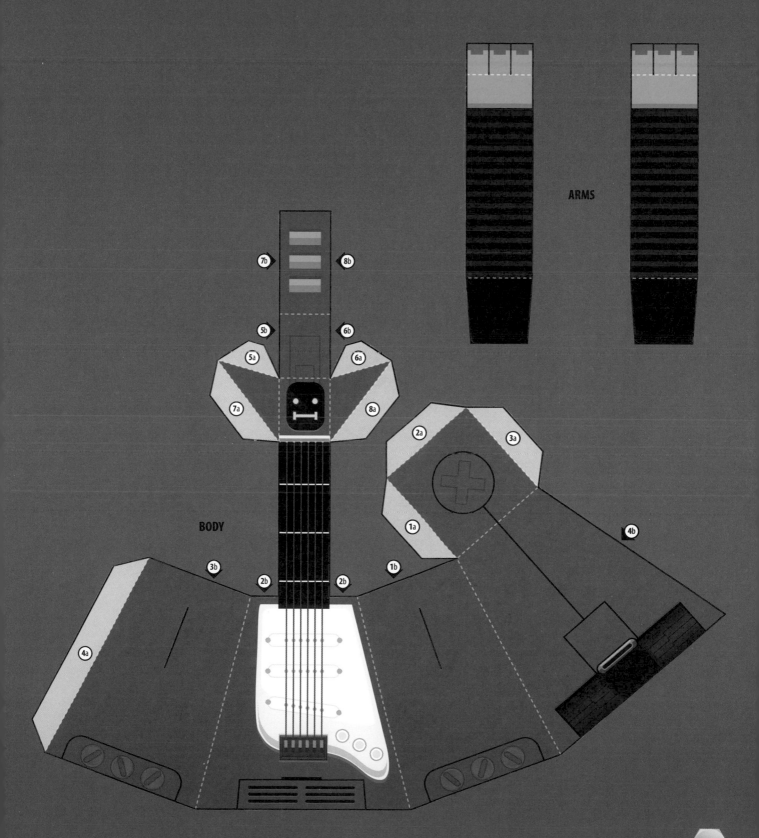

ARMS

7b 8b

5b 6b

5a 6a

7a 8a

2a 3a

1a

4b

BODY

3b

2b 2b

1b

4a

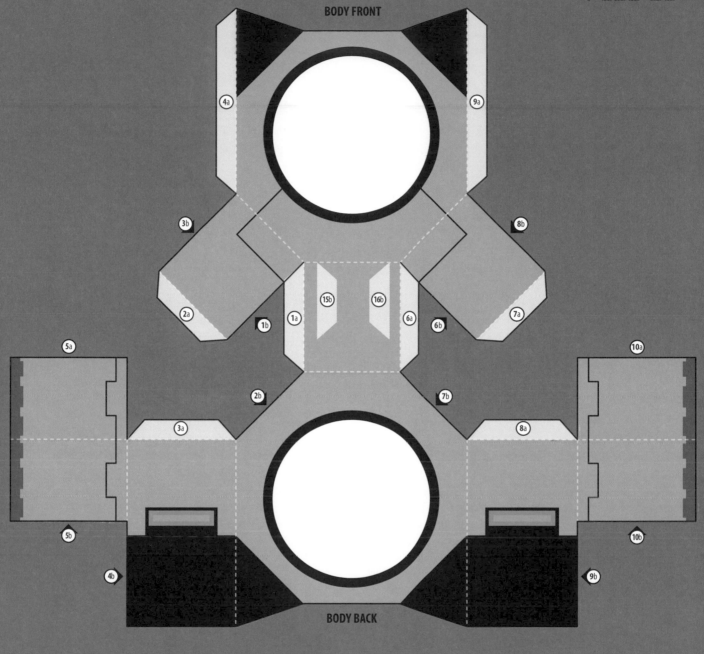

BODY FRONT

BODY BACK

HEAD

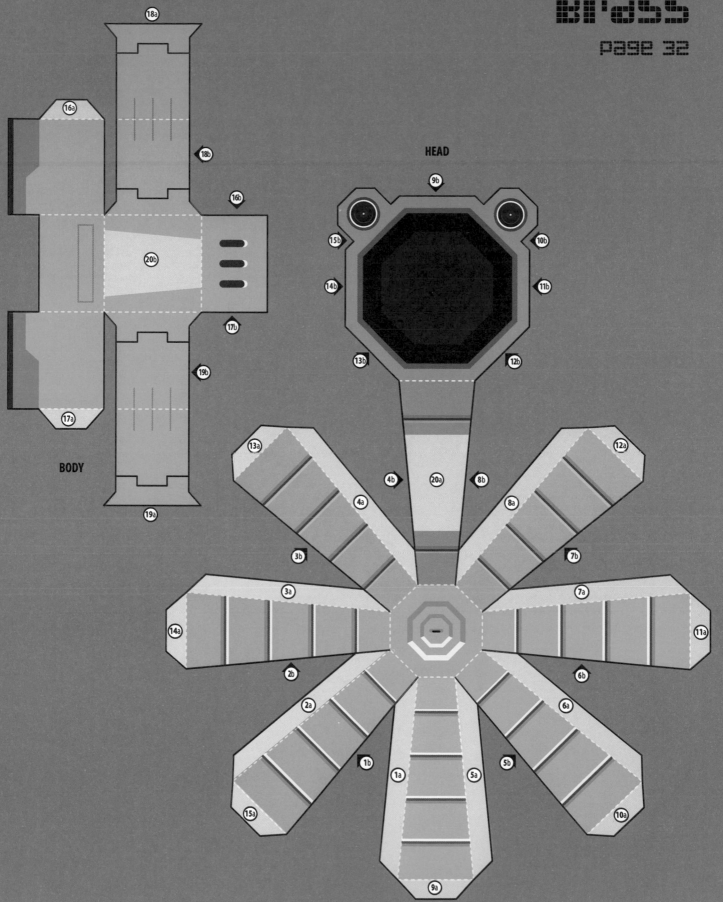

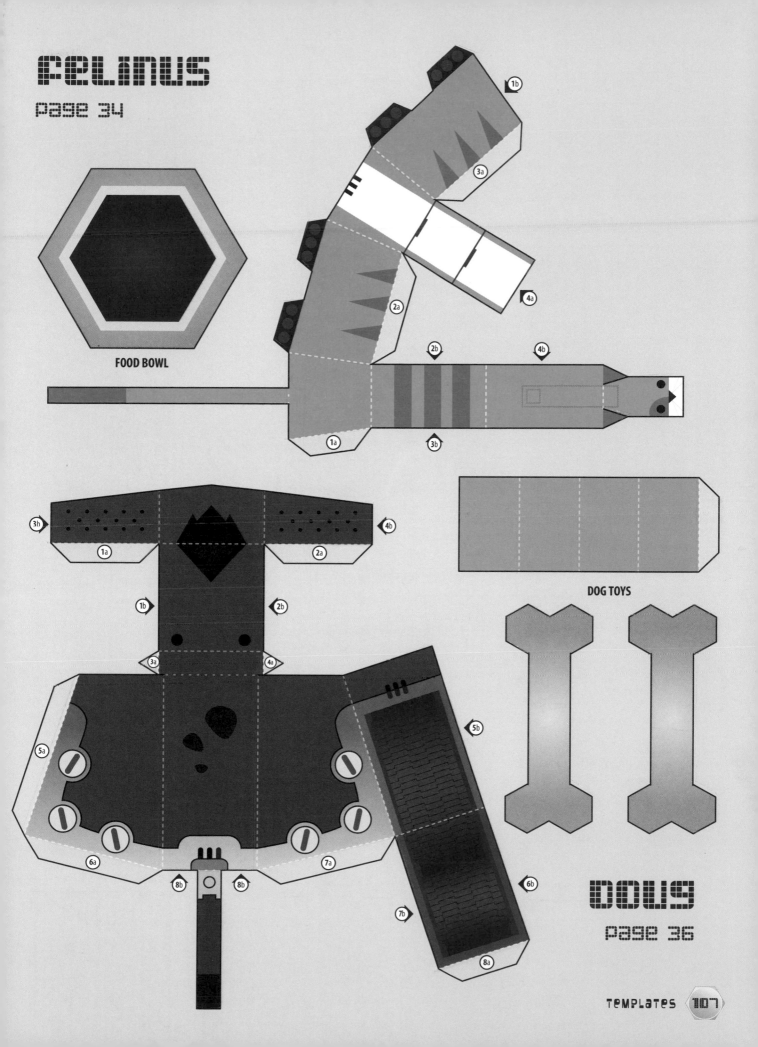

PELINUS
page 34

FOOD BOWL

DOG TOYS

DOUS
page 36

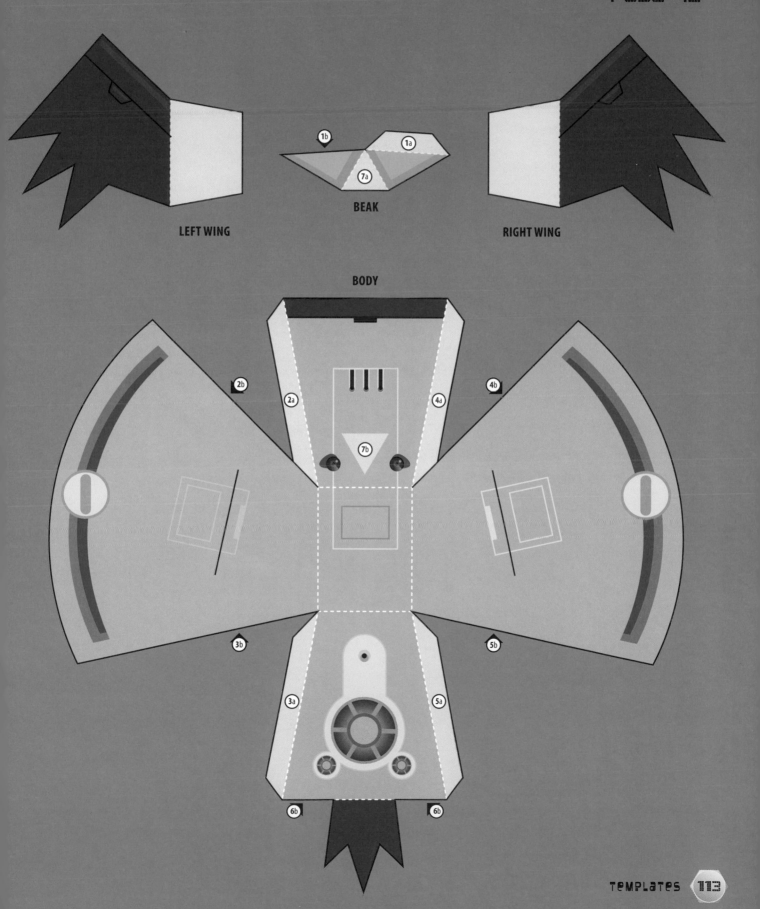

LEFT WING

BEAK

RIGHT WING

BODY

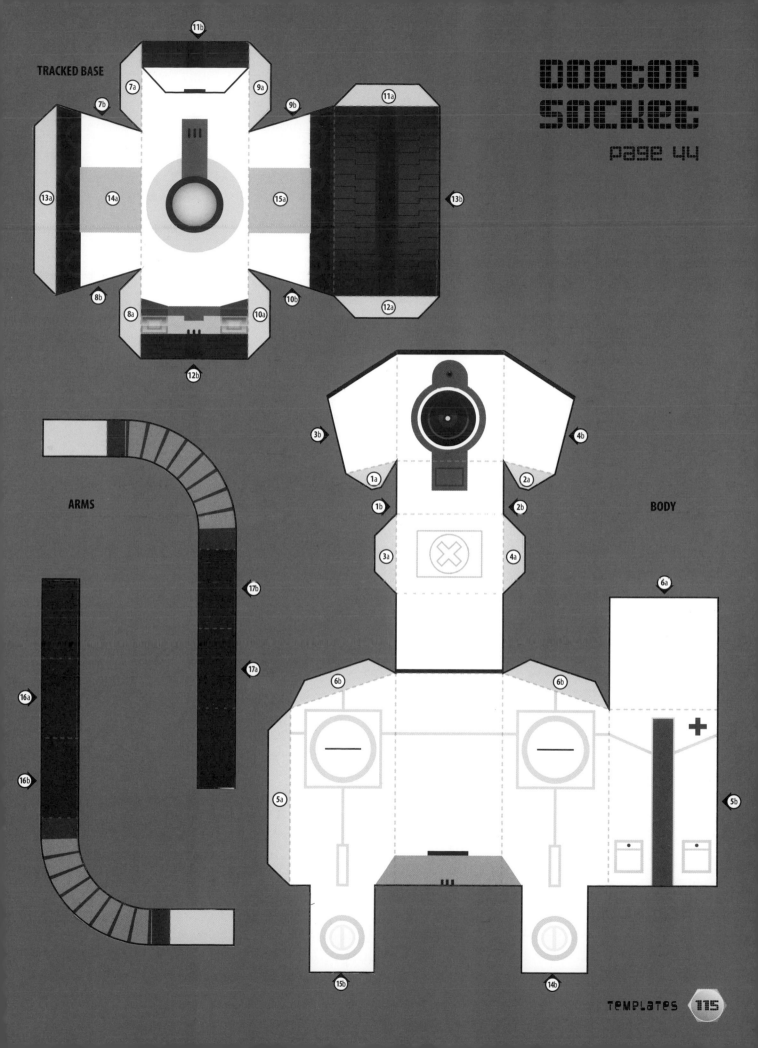

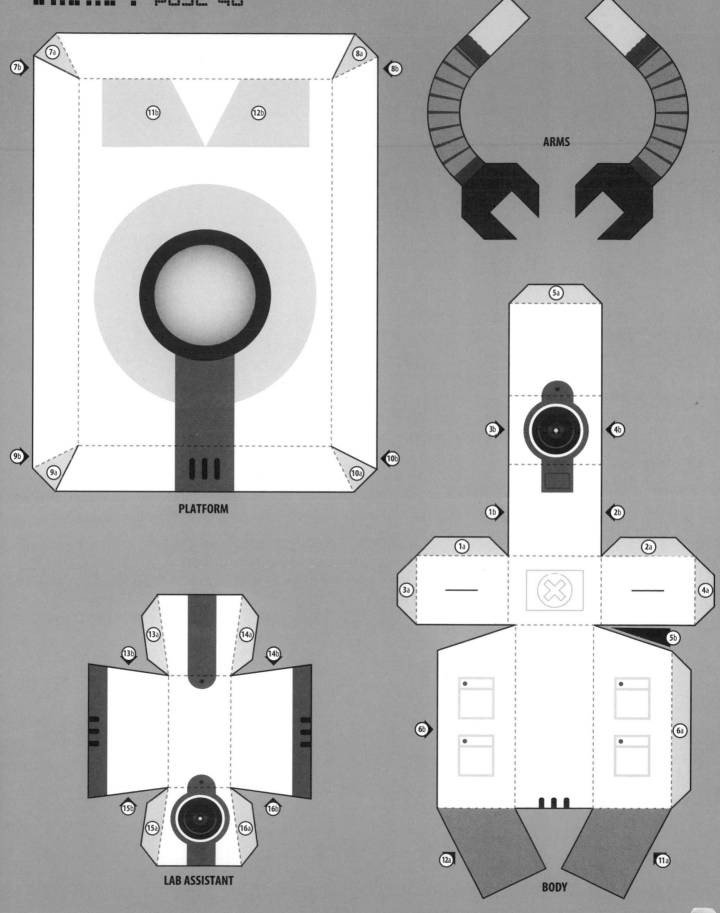

PLATFORM

ARMS

BODY

LAB ASSISTANT

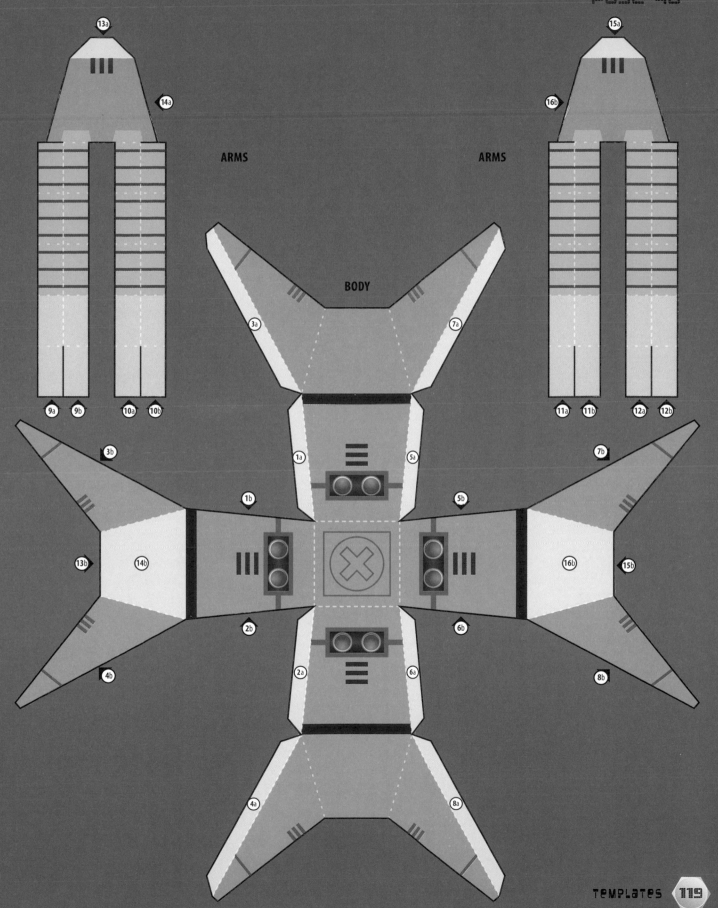

ARMS

ARMS

BODY

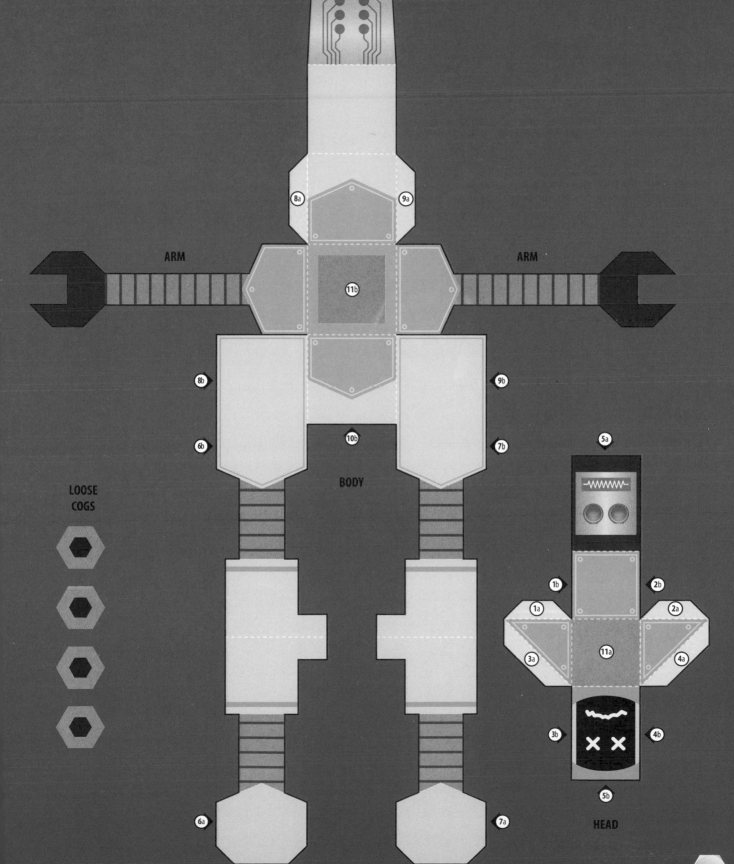

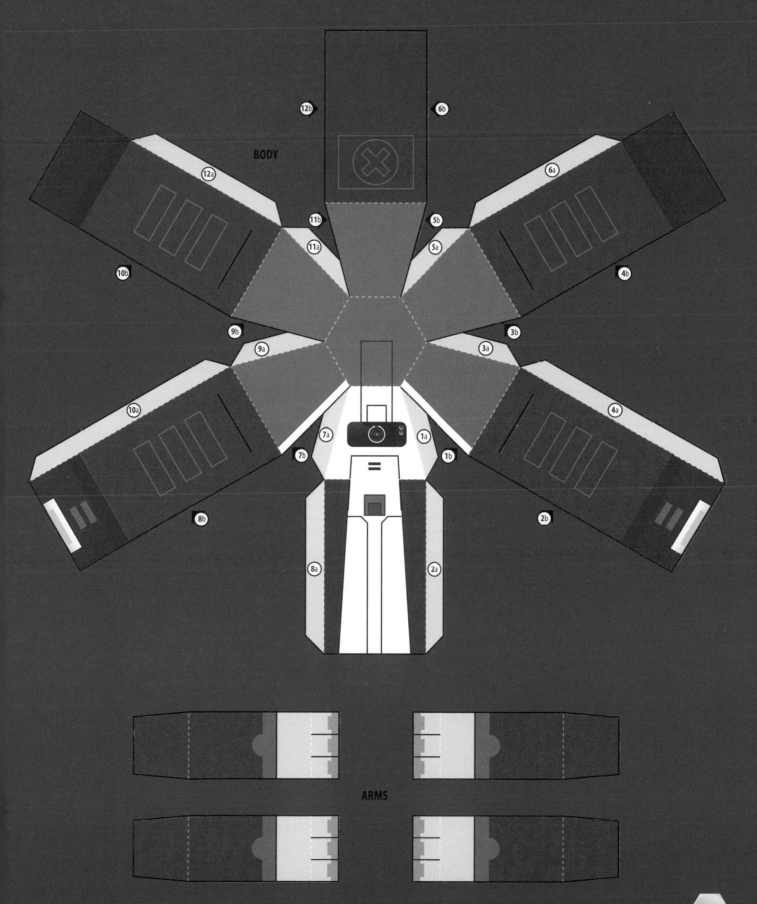

BODY

ARMS

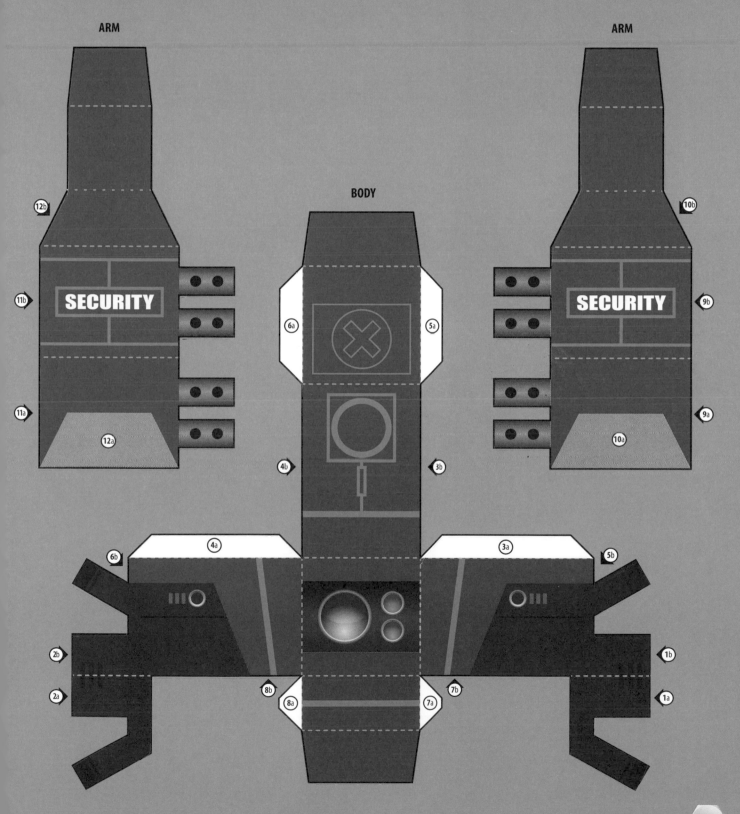

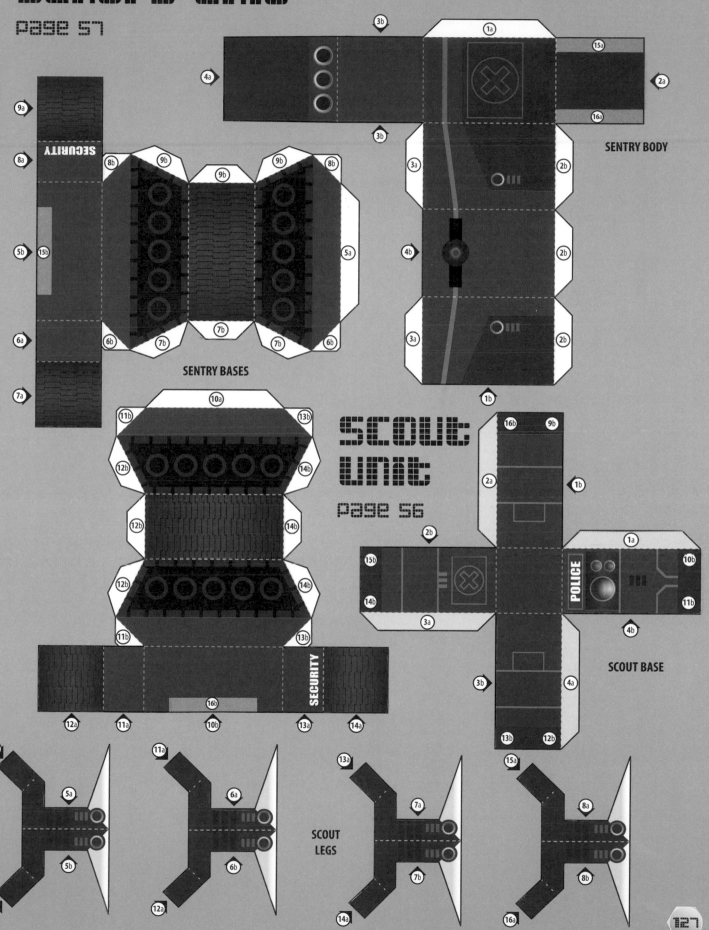

sentry unit
page 57

SENTRY BODY

SENTRY BASES

SECURITY

scout unit
page 56

SCOUT BASE

SCOUT LEGS

SECURITY

POLICE

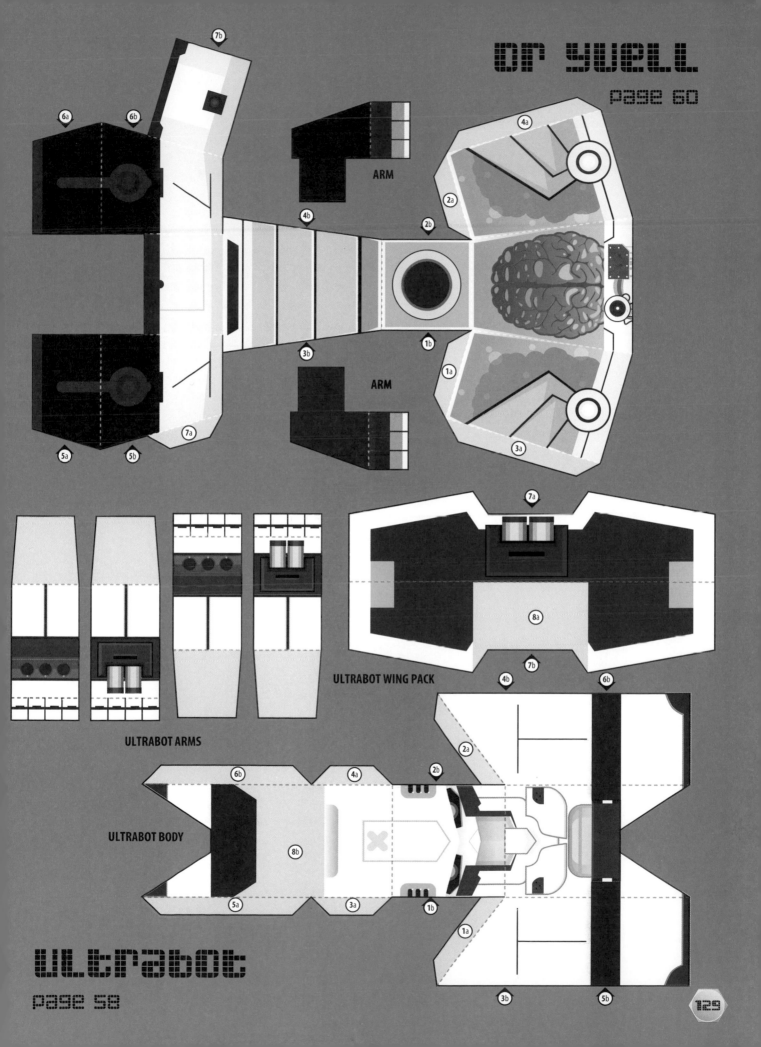

ARM

ARM

ULTRABOT WING PACK

ULTRABOT ARMS

ULTRABOT BODY

Ultrabot
page 58

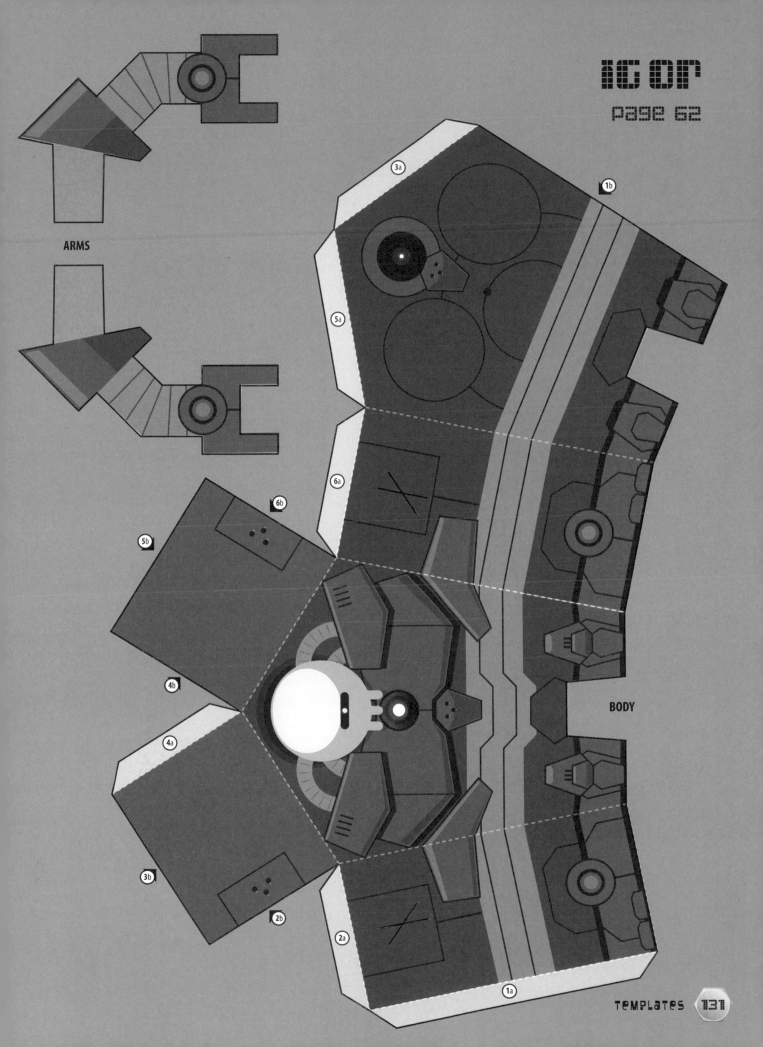

ARMS

BODY

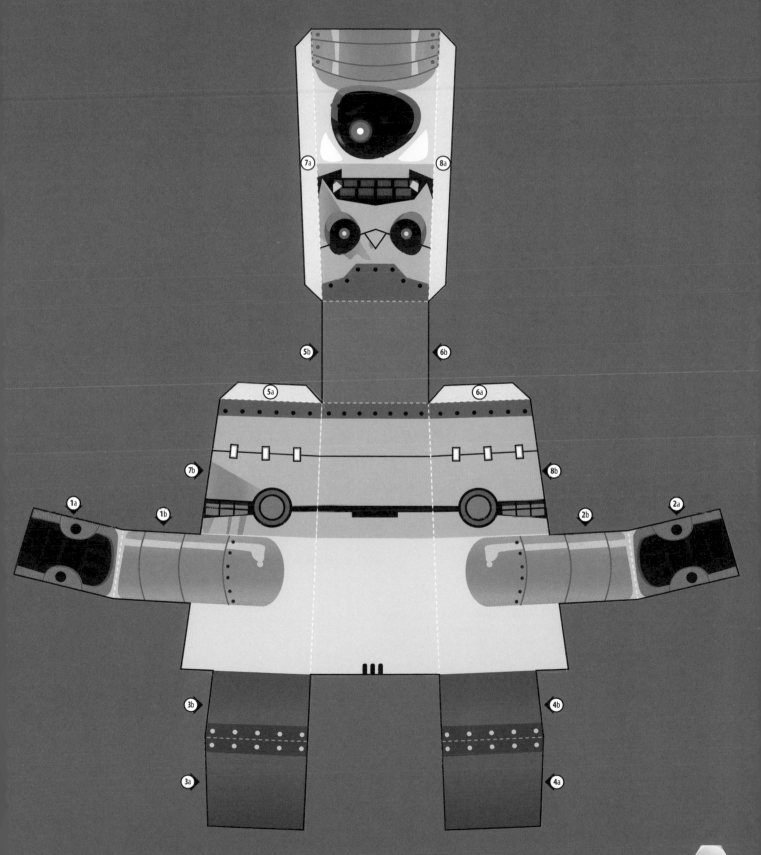

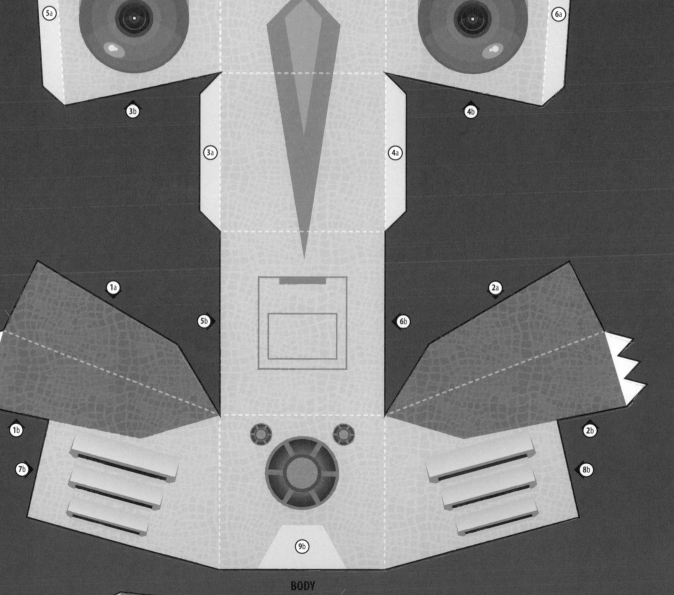

BODY

TAIL

ROBORILLA

BODY

HEAD

ARM 1

ARM 2

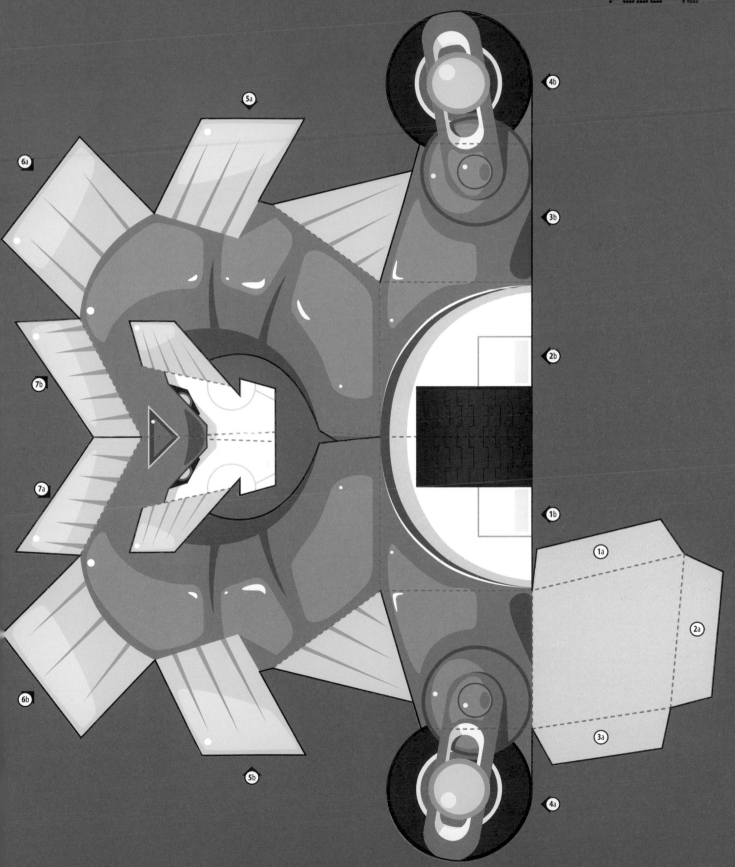

5a
6a
4b
3b
2b
7b
7a
1b
1a
2a
6b
5b
4a
3a

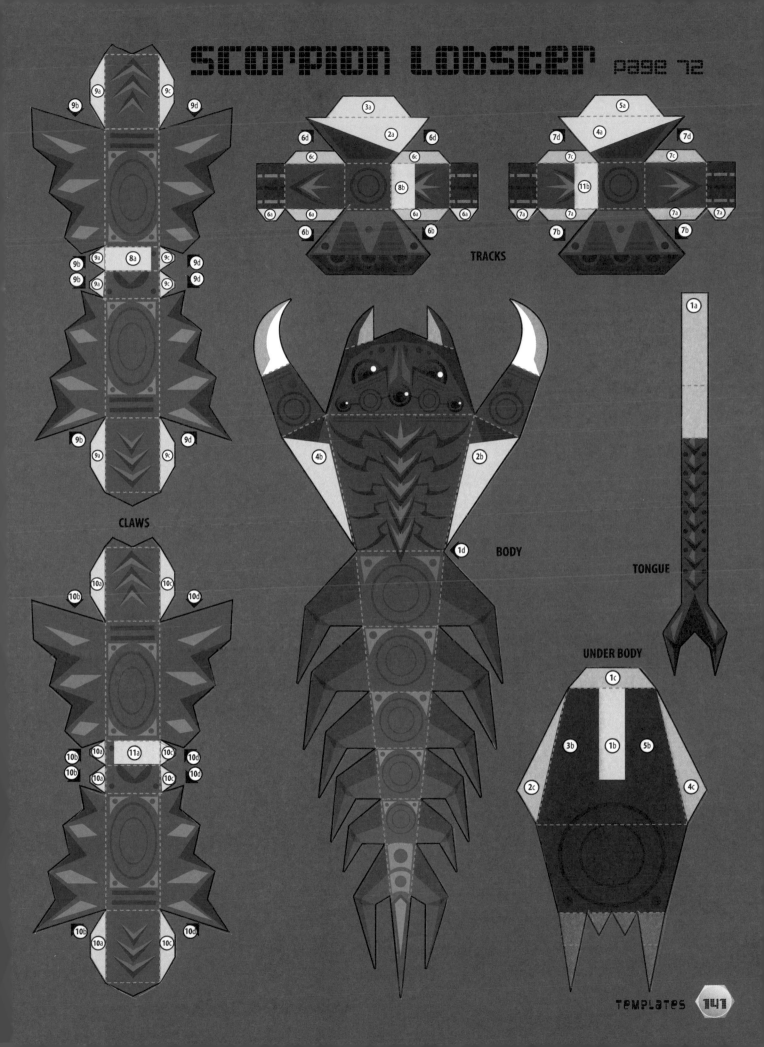

CLAWS

TRACKS

BODY

TONGUE

UNDER BODY